T0162995

The Italian Journals

Peter Greco and Dean D'Adamo

Where to Go, What to Eat and Who to Leave at Home

iUniverse, Inc.
Bloomington

The Italian Journals
Where to Go, What to Eat and Who to Leave at Home

iUniverse books may be ordered through booksellers or by contacting:

iUniverse
1663 Liberty Drive
Bloomington, IN 47403
www.iuniverse.com
1-800-Authors (1-800-288-4677)

Because of the dynamic nature of the Internet, any Web addresses or links contained in this book may have changed since publication and may no longer be valid. The views expressed in this work are solely those of the author and do not necessarily reflect the views of the publisher, and the publisher hereby disclaims any responsibility for them.

Any people depicted in stock imagery provided by Thinkstock are models, and such images are being used for illustrative purposes only.

Certain stock imagery © Thinkstock.

ISBN: 978-1-4697-0006-9 (sc)
ISBN: 978-1-4697-0007-6 (e)

Printed in the United States of America

iUniverse rev. date: 1/13/2012

CONTENTS

INTRODUCTION

This is a story; a pair of stories actually, about a vacation. While you read this book and laugh in disbelief at the various incidents, please keep in mind that it is almost completely true. A few names have been altered because I'm convinced that the individuals involved could have me killed. But, by and large, everything that is reported, happened, at least in the eyes of the authors.

The crux of this tale stems from one question. Can two couples go to Italy for two weeks and blissfully enjoy the history, natural beauty and each other without frustration, aggravation, and turmoil? The answer is yes, provided none of the people involved is Dean "Dino" D'Adamo. There are a lot of adjectives I can apply to my Italian vacation with Dino and his wife Cathy. You will read many of them over the ensuing pages, but if you find any form of the word "bliss" anywhere, congratulations, you have a rare misprinted copy.

My wife, Carolyn, and I had long talked about going to Italy. When we finally got the opportunity, it turned out we were fated to go with another couple, the D'Adamos (pronounced *dee ah DAHM oh*). The trip was also going to be a vehicle for my first book. I've had some humorous articles published in various newspapers and magazines and have performed comedy in clubs and corporate events. Over the years I had several ideas for books. Most of these were autobiographical and no matter how entertaining they might be, very few people have any reason to read about my life. So writing a book about a trip to Italy struck me as a good angle. Plus, as it turned out, a friend of mine was tight with a literary agent who was going to be in Venice just about the time our trip would be ending there. The agent had agreed to meet with me and review my story outline to see if it was something he could sell. I didn't have a premise for the book when we set off for Italy, but I figured once I got there and soaked up the culture and the sites, I would have plenty of time to produce an outline. I was naively confident that a theme would simply emerge as a matter of evolution. Well, somewhere Charles Darwin is laughing his ass off.

The raw material for my book was to be mined from a journal I would keep throughout the trip. I wanted to keep a journal even if there wasn't a book so I could clearly remember the sites, sounds and interesting occurrences. None of the three people I was traveling with were the note-taking type and what each of us was likely to commit to memory differed greatly. For example, Cathy would remember the stores. Carolyn would remember different stores. And Dino...well, let me give you an analogy. You know those trick pictures where one person sees a pretty girl and somebody else sees an old lady? That pretty much describes how differently Dino and I see things, except in this case it would be more like one person sees a pretty girl and the other person sees my head exploding. If I depended on Dino's recollection, I would end up thinking we visited one of the rings of Saturn for two weeks instead of Rome, Florence and Venice. So if I was going to have accurate information for personal or literary use, I would need to provide it myself.

I have a kind of academic curiosity about the people, places and things I experience when I travel; almost like a wildlife photographer blending in with the surroundings so as not to intrude on the normal flow of the environment. Dino, on the other hand, approached this vacation the way he approaches everything in life; the way a Great Dane approaches a barbecue. "There's meat! I like meat. I want meat. I'm taking meat. That meat was good! Why are these people chasing me? If I enjoyed the meat so much, how can they be angry? Why is my owner locking me in the laundry room...again?" Dino wants what he wants and can't understand why everybody else doesn't instinctively accommodate him. I, on the other hand, like people. So you can imagine how different our views of the trip would be. And so, for reasons which will be explained later, Dino's day by day account of the trip is included along with my story.

On one thing we readily agreed; Italy is magnificent. As a "bonus" I hope the descriptions included herein will be helpful for those planning such a trip or provide a nostalgic look for those who have already been there. Even if you are not planning to visit Italy, I hope you will get an appreciation for this wonderful country. I also added some pictures and ignored any rational suggestions from my wife, just like I did when we were in Italy. The result is one part guide to enjoying Rome, Florence and Venice, and two parts examination of human interaction that will set the study of sociology back fifty years. Dino says forty-nine.

Peter Greco

PART 1: HOW DID THIS HAPPEN?

You will notice throughout this story that I love to eat. So it is oddly appropriate that this entire adventure began with a chat over dinner. It makes me think that many similarly ill-fated events probably sprung from an exchange at a meal. I can imagine Julius Caesar poking at a squab on his plate and suggesting to his wife that maybe he would get his good toga from the dry cleaners and head on down to the Senate to meet with Brutus and the rest of the guys. Hell, half the people on the Titanic were probably still at the midnight buffet when the first alarm went off. I'm too good a Catholic to mention the Last Supper, but isn't it possible that Jefferson Davis and a few pals were tucking into some barbecue when somebody offhandedly suggested it wouldn't be such a big deal to split off from the Union? So it was for my wife Carolyn and me, when we went out to dinner with the D'Adamos. Four people having a nice dinner in an Italian restaurant in South Florida. One minute we're ordering drinks and talking about our kids and the next thing I know, they're serving appetizers and I'm being asked whether I want to start the trip in Rome or Venice.

You might think, "What's the big deal? Lots of people get the idea to travel together over dinner." True, very true, but those are people who enjoy, or can imagine enjoying, extended periods of time together. While that concept holds true for Carolyn, Cathy and I, it completely falls apart when Dino is added to the equation. To get the whole picture, I'll need to tell you something about the four of us. So, we'll interrupt this dinner story to give you some background.

Things were going so well…

It all started at work. I met Carolyn there, and we got married eighteen months after our first date. Speed was essential, since I correctly figured that Carolyn would eventually realize she could do better than me. Every other girl I had dated had come to the same conclusion by about the third month of the relationship. My timing was extraordinarily good in this case. Carolyn was unattached at the time since her most recent suitor had moved away for a job. Our first date went very well. I know because I had her complete a questionnaire when I dropped her off that night. I proposed after six weeks, just before we got to the point where I began repeating my eleven hilarious stories. As I popped the question she did some quick calculations. On the one hand, there was probably a better looking, more successful guy out there if she waited. But on the other hand she saw potential. She was intrigued. Like most wives, Carolyn viewed her husband as a project which, with a certain amount of work and regardless of the raw material, could be customized to her exact specifications. When it came to me, her friends were divided into two camps. Half of them viewed me as an impossible mission that was doomed to end in failure. These women felt that I didn't sufficiently value important things like clothing, houses, personal grooming, and other trappings of a "successful" life. They considered me a nice enough, happy-go-lucky idealist (code words for "date don't marry"). The other half of Carolyn's friends saw me as a potentially epic achievement. If Carolyn could transform me into somebody who was happy *and* "successful", she would be Nobel Prize material.

I had one thing in my favor. As a kid, I carefully observed my parents' marriage. Certainly they loved each other, but there were regular skirmishes on a variety of topics, for example did we have to panel *every* room in the house!? Dad was a fighter, but ultimately, after about twenty years and an involuntary weekend at Marriage Encounter he ran up the white flag. Just before my wedding, he took me aside and gave me advice for the first time ever. He said, "It's not your house, it's not your money, it's not your anything. It's all hers. If there's something you really want, make it *her* idea."

I may be slow, but I'm not completely stupid. I took my Dad's advice and soon discovered I was happier than any married man I knew. It took two years and several dozen blows to the male pride, but it worked. Whatever was important to Carolyn, I gave her. And if something was important to me, I simply mentioned it as something I was vaguely interested in or aware of, and eventually she found herself encouraging me to have it, do it, eat it, or wear it, mostly out of guilt for having things so much better than any wife she knew. It had to frustrate the hell out of Carolyn, but what could she do? She ran out of things to fix with me, and found little satisfaction in her victory. It must have been like a boxer who trains for months for a title fight and the other guy ends up throwing in the towel while the referee goes over the pre-fight instructions. You won, but you still want to hit something.

She keeps working on me, although I think it is mostly out of habit or instinct at this point. I remain vigilant because if I get complacent I know I will be given new challenges in new areas, like child-rearing or bookkeeping. It's a pleasant, relaxed, but alert relationship. She's got a husband she can't complain about, and I've got a wife.

I'll take Italian Dictators for $100, Alex

Shortly after we got married, Cathy came to work at the same company. She and Carolyn hit it off right away and Cathy worked for me in the engineering group. Shortly after that move, we hired Dino as a salesman. One of my jobs was to go on calls with the sales reps and answer any questions more technical than, "How much?" Those of us who did engineering had a natural mistrust of salesmen, so I was wary of Dino as we made our first sales call.

The forty-minute car ride had been completely silent, except early on when Dino told me I had should have taken a different route that would have saved fifteen minutes. A half hour later, while driving wordlessly through South Jersey we saw a diner, a common site in this part of the country. But this one was different. There was no lighting around it, no flashy advertising. There was just a four-foot-high, one-word sign on the roof announcing "Food." Dino looked at the sign, thought for a second, and broke the silence saying, "Food is good." Okay, so maybe this guy had at least one redeeming characteristic.

Food *is* good. There are those who eat to live and those who live to eat. I live to eat—almost exclusively. My wife comes from a family of eight kids and things were tight growing up. Sometimes they ate navy beans on bread for dinner, so what does she know about eating? My family had one used car and we went on a week's vacation about five times in the seventeen years I lived at home. But food was a big deal. My mom had a rotation of about fifteen main courses. There were some clunkers to be sure. Ham butt and waxed beans, otherwise known as the sodium missile with a side of nausea, was eminently forgettable. But her beef stew, rolled flank steak, and spaghetti were epic, and by my teens I was already learning to cook.

Dino professed his love of food and opened the floodgates of conversation. The sales call we were going on lasted about ten minutes. I broke all my rules and just agreed to give the guy what he wanted for whatever he wanted to pay. I would figure out if we could actually do that later. We hustled back into the car and talked more about food. I brought up music, but Dino said everybody but Sinatra and Motown sucked, so I went right back to food. Dino's theories on eating were completely different from mine. Dino ate whatever he wanted, not just what happened to be in the house. If he wanted the last piece of something, he took it—right away, no politely asking if somebody else wants it first. He believed people should respect food. At Halloween he gave out toast. What did these kids do to deserve candy; wear a costume? Not enough. I was infatuated with the guy's passion. But there were subtle signs of danger here, like an invitation to a taco eating contest; tempting at first, but , all too easy to overlook the side effects. For example, to say he is opinionated is like saying Jesus sounds like a nice guy. He is always willing to share his opinions and thoughts, and you are welcome to agree with him. Added to this is the fact that, physically, he is pretty imposing. Dino is a longtime weightlifter, and every once in a while he will suddenly, involuntarily twitch or flex something. When he does this, you would swear he's about to smack you. So when you talk to him you find yourself simultaneously nodding in agreement and shooting your hand out to protect against a phantom left hook.

What puzzled Carolyn and me, and everybody else at work, was the basis for the attraction between Dino and Cathy. Sure, they are both good-looking people, they both have strong core values, and they each obviously wanted to be with somebody who could take a joke. But Cathy is stylish and gracious, with sophisticated tastes. The living room in Dino's bachelor pad featured a barber's chair, a Universal Gym and an old fashioned Coke machine adapted to dispense seven ounce bottles of beer. What brings people like this together? Carolyn and I thought about asking them a number of times, but she believes that thinking about that would just send Cathy into an emotional tailspin. I think if you asked Dino he would say, "I don't know, but she's one lucky broad."

A little less than a year after Dino started working with us, and over the objections and amazement of everyone who knew Cathy, they started dating. And the day after Thanksgiving 1986, they got married. Until around 1994, friends had to point out to Dino that his anniversary wasn't the day after Thanksgiving every year. Things like anniversaries, birthdays, and his children's names aren't the kinds of things he keeps track of; those are his idea of what wives and mothers are for. Dino would say that makes him a classic man's man. Me? I can tell you where Carolyn and I sat, at which restaurant, what we ate, and what she laughed at, on our first date. Dino would say that makes me a man's woman.

When Dino and Cathy were first married we would usually see each other at company events, such as Christmas parties and picnics. Dino liked limiting his exposure to us (me, actually) to these events where he had the option of talking to other people. One day Carolyn and I were driving in the D'Adamos neighborhood and decided to pop in for an unannounced visit. Two weeks later, Dino took a new job and transferred to Fairfield, Connecticut. We visited them there one weekend and two weeks after that visit they moved to Atlanta. Cathy asked that we not visit them in Atlanta because she feared Dino would then make her move to Ecuador.

On one occasion, Dino and I once had earned Caribbean cruise for ourselves and our wives as part of a recognition event. When we got to the cruise ship, Carolyn and I discovered we'd been assigned a nice little cabin with a bed, a chair, and a sliding door that opened to a balcony about the size of an appliance box. We invited Dino and Cathy to come to our cabin to have a drink before dinner. They showed up at our room, and Dino's jaw dropped. Evidently their cabin didn't have a chair or a sliding door or a ... whaaaat theee fuck?!! A balcony!? In fact, their accommodations consisted of a bed completely hemmed in by four walls, and a toilet, sink, and shower nozzle tucked into a closet. Dino was dumbfounded. His defining trait is his lack of a diplomatic editor in his head. Instead of saying something like, "Hey, you guys really lucked out on the room. Ours is a sardine can!" he said, "How the fuck did you guys get a room like this instead of me?" For the rest of the cruise, Dino couldn't get away from the size of the cabins. We were having drinks at a bar, and he said, "I swear to God, that bartender gave you more booze than me. Just like the fucking cabin!" Oh yeah, I should add, Dino curses ... all the time. That thing you are sitting on right now? It's called a fucking chair. I think he even spells it that way when he writes it down. And that's how he talks when he's *not* upset.

For the rest of the cruise, I tried to avoid Dino, but it was a small ship and there was only one buffet line. When the trip was over, the girls suggested planning a trip together some day. They said this when Dino was out of earshot. He was committed to never traveling with us ever again, especially if balconies were involved.

It doesn't help that Dino is a certified member of Mensa. My suspicion is that he miraculously hit the right pattern of "a," "b," "c," and "d" answers when he took the test, but nevertheless, he can document his intellectual status. So that is the basis for Dino's relationships. We appreciate how hard it must be for a genius to endure morons like us, and in return Dino accepts people in spite of their mental deficiencies. He is both omniscient and tolerant.

Back to Dinner

So, now that you have a little clearer picture of the participants, let's go back to dinner.

Dino and I happened to be in our Florida offices for separate meetings. Because our kids were old enough to be left alone, each of our wives had coincidentally joined us for the trip. (Point of clarification: To me, "old enough to be left alone" meant our youngest was nineteen and away at college. Dino has no idea how old his kids are, but they can feed themselves, so he figures, "What the hell? You think if the plane crashed and I died they couldn't get along without me for a couple of fucking days? I mean, the house is full of fucking food, and they get a couple of days off from fucking school. Everybody wins. What the fuck").

Reluctantly Dino agreed to the idea of the four of us having dinner together. *He* was reluctant. So we let Dino pick the restaurant, pick where we sat and what we would share as appetizers.

The evening was moving along pleasantly until I mentioned that our daughter Jackie, an art major, was thinking about going to Italy for a semester. That led to the discovery that each of us had been interested in going to Italy some day. The wives exploded with talk of the things they wanted to see and do. They were moving far faster on this than Dino or I. For his part, Dino seemed a little subdued. You could tell he liked the idea; liked the thought of having me as a foil for this adventure, but at the same time he was mentally cataloging all my shortcomings and how they would impact his ability to enjoy the trip.

Dino's lack of enthusiasm was nothing compared to mine. I had long dreamed of going to Italy. As soon as Jackie mentioned taking a semester there I began to think we could visit her and maybe I could write a book about the trip. That would require some time alone and if Carolyn was spending time with Jackie, I would be freed up to think and write. But adding Dino would be a significant complication.

As Cathy and Carolyn got more animated, so did Dino. If I didn't act quickly, this was going to get out of control. What could I do? Using my Political Science degree for the first time, I diplomatically and politely alluded to some potential complications. "Are you women insane? You're talking about putting Dino in charge of our lives for two weeks! That's the worst idea I have ever heard!" But, evidently that was too subtle. Then I thought I would just wait and when Dino eventually said something ridiculous the wives would be snapped back to their senses. But even when he flatly stated that Cathy could only bring one suitcase and two pairs of shoes, she was completely undeterred. We were screwed. Didn't the girls realize this?

By the time we were sipping Sambuca, it was no longer a theoretical discussion. We were going to Italy with the D'Adamos in September while Jackie would be in Florence. When we got back to our hotel room that evening, the conversation went like this

Peter: "You know you just committed us to go to Italy with Dino."

Carolyn: "…and Cathy. You like Cathy, don't you?"

Peter: "Of Course I do. But it's Dino, Carolyn…Dino. If anything goes wrong he'll beat me up…if I'm lucky"

Carolyn: "Oh come on. He likes you…he…really…he doesn't hate you…he…You like Cathy, right? .

Over the next couple of months we had calls with the D'Adamos to firm up the date, the duration and the cities we would visit. We had a couple of calls to discuss arrangements and assign tasks. Cathy stepped up big time and handled details like hotels, transportation, logistics, a couple of one-day tours, and major sites to see. The amount and quality of information she gathered was very impressive. In spite of Dino telling her what was stupid and what was OK, she was able to put together an ideal itinerary. We would go to Rome, Florence and Venice over a span of 15 days. Dino said he would handle the language issues; evidently he believed his inability to get along with people in English made him goodwill ambassador to Italy. I was assigned responsibility for knowing the history and other details about the country. This left Carolyn. Dino loves Carolyn because he can bust her chops and she'll just laugh and give it right back to him. When it came to having Carolyn take on part of the arrangements, Dino just paused and said, "We'll get back to you on that." He noted that this was a big trip that would cost lots of money, and that we couldn't afford any screw-ups, so maybe we should keep Carolyn out of the planning effort altogether. After some more jabs, Carolyn suggested that she could arrange the Vatican tour. Dino's response: "I'm not Catholic, so what the hell. Knock yourself out."

The trip was on. I had two months to get myself psyched.

How the Hell Did This Happen?? According to Dino

Once upon a time I went to work at a company that sold telephone systems. Since I was very familiar with phones, having used them since I was a kid, I figured I was ideally qualified for the position and so did the guy I interviewed with because after an hour of discussing why the N.Y. Giants should change their name to the New Jersey Giants, he offered me the job. That's where I met Peter Greco. He was the engineering manager and I was forced to consult with him before visiting customers, after which I immediately disregarded everything he said. It was either that or let some other lying sales guy win the deal. I was pretty damn successful by following a simple strategy with every account: mention the opportunity to Peter; think about what I'm going to buy with the commission while he tells me what not to do; nod enthusiastically when he looks like he might be saying something important; then go and do whatever the hell I think it's going to take to win the business. Sounds easy and it was. My career in the telecom biz was off and running. Life was good; nuthin' but blue skies. That is until a certain little Asian babe caught my eye and the clouds came rolling in. Not at first of course. At first things were great. Here was this exotically beautiful sales engineer who paid for her own lunch and laughed at my jokes. Then, in what seemed like the blink of a slanted eye, my jokes were no longer funny and I was just another married sales guy wondering how one thin slice of wedding cake could simultaneously erase a woman's libido and her sense of humor. Before I knew it, my hot, yet suddenly unapproachable, Asian trophy wife had me socializing with the guy who I'd spent the last two years ignoring, Peter Greco, along with his big haired trophy wife, Carolyn. So now I'm forced to sit at tables in crowded restaurants divulging very personal information that I'm uncomfortable sharing like what I'm having for dinner and how I liked my appetizer. For all intents and purposes I now am reduced to viewing my life in the side view mirror. I'd use the rear view but Carolyn is sitting in the back seat and her huge hair is in the way.

To be completely fair, I must admit that despite everything, Peter is basically a good guy, one of the most intelligent and humble people I know. Of course, Pete has a lot to be humble about, so I guess that really shouldn't count for a hell of a lot. I truly believe that the guy has potential; he's just too insecure to tap it. He generally acts like he's embarrassed by my behavior but I think that secretly, down deep in places that Pete's conscious mind has convinced him don't exist, he wishes he could be more like me...honest, courageous and self assured. On Pete's conscious level however, my wonderful traits have become twisted and sinister. That's how Pete sees me, because to admit otherwise would make his jealousy unbearable and therefore he actually invents bizarre versions of actual incidents that make me look opinionated, insensitive and selfish. At least that's how I see it.

Tonight, Cathy and I are in south Florida and so are the Grecos and somehow, someone decided that we would all go out to dinner together. I figure, what the hell? Worst case if things really get boring I can say something that will outrage politically liberal Carolyn and get her to snort wine out of her nose. It takes careful timing but it can be done.

Both Grecos are nice people, which is not my favorite kind because they almost make me feel like I have to be nice too... almost. I really don't mind going to dinner with them once in a while, but tonight the discussion somehow focuses on how all of us wanted to visit the old country. Pretty soon I could see where this was headed and before I knew it knew it the girls had decided that we would all embark on a two-week trip to Italy. Cathy and Carolyn were talking over each other suggesting dates and landmarks they'd want to see. I haven't seen Cathy so excited since... Actually, I've never seen her this excited. I really want to go to Italy; almost as much as I don't want to go on vacation with the Grecos. I just sat there not saying much, figuring I would be able to talk my wife out of it later. Didn't work. So I'm now going to Italy for two weeks with the Grecos. I thought it would end badly (and had a sneaking suspicion that it would also start badly and continue badly). But after a good deal of soul searching, I came to the conclusion that the old axiom "Whatever doesn't kill me only makes me stronger" was probably true. As long as I could survive those two weeks, I would probably return with arms the size of Serena Williams. So I finally resigned myself to the idea, confident that with the proper amount of mental conditioning, I could survive it.

I inform Cathy that I'm in, but it's conditional on a couple of nonnegotiable items. First, she doesn't say a thing to me regarding the amount of alcohol I consume. She agrees. Second, I insist that if we're going, we're going to be prepared, which means everyone is going to have a pre-trip job. And I get to "assign" everyone their responsibilities. To this she says nothing, which I take as another yes. So I sit down and e-mail everybody, including my wife, everyone's responsibilities. Cathy's job is to research all accommodations, choose the sites we definitely want to see, and make all arrangements. I'm to learn the language. Not to be fluent—just enough to get by. Peter is supposed to study the history of Italy and understand the interesting facts about the sites we will visit. And Carolyn; well Carolyn's job is—OK, I have to be careful here. I give her a couple of things to handle, none of the important stuff, just enough so she will feel like she's contributing. I can't exactly say why, but Carolyn has never instilled me with a lot of confidence in her, and I am not about to risk screwing up this vacation just because I don't want to offend her, especially since I generally go out of my way just to offend her.

Now I realize that Pete and Carolyn think that I'm a control freak and that I always have to be in charge of things, but they're wrong. I'm not a control freak. I merely want to make sure that if I'm involved in something, especially something as important as this trip, things don't get all screwed up because someone didn't do something because they thought someone else was handling something, and pretty soon so many somethings fall between the cracks that it winds up being a huge cluster. And by the way, if someone else besides me wants to take ownership to make sure things go smoothly, I'm overjoyed. In fact, I prefer that someone else does it, but in this case, knowing the other three like I do, that role obviously falls on my shoulders. So, as usual (*come al solito*), I don't care what the others think, and at least with me in charge there's no question that everything will go well and everybody will have the best damn vacation they ever had ... if it fucking kills them.

For the next couple of months, Cathy is really focused on her responsibility, spending an hour or two every night researching and blogging every detail of the trip, from how many days we should spend in each major city to where we can find the best prices on souvenirs (her definition of souvenirs being shoes, dresses, and leather boots for herself, and postcards for everyone else). She also finds and books a guide to take us to Cinque Terre, Siena, Lucca, and a few other places in Tuscany. While Cathy is busy earning an A in her class, "Making Sure You Don't Screw Up Your Husband's Vacation - 101," I'm sure that neither of the Grecos has even cracked a book yet.

I, however, have cracked a few books (of Italian words and phrases), and read them every chance I get, which is pretty often because I keep them in the magazine stand next to the toilet. I find myself learning new words every day, and after a particularly spicy rack of barbecued ribs one night, eight new phrases and the proper conjugation of eleven verbs. As the day of our departure looms, I can only hope that the Grecos are holding up their end of the bargain, but I am damn certain that they're not.

PART 2: ROME: I KNOW LESS ABOUT THE VATICAN NOW THAN I DID BEFORE WE GOT HERE

Tuesday, September 9: Peter's Version

My son dropped Carolyn and I off at Philadelphia International Airport at 4 in the afternoon, Dino and Cathy would be flying out of Atlanta about a half hour earlier than us. We went to the CIBA bar/restaurant in the International Terminal and split some cornbread-crusted Portobello mushrooms and a couple of beers. As I was writing that down, Carolyn asked, "You aren't going to write down everything we eat for the next two weeks are you?" I looked at her blankly, hesitated for about three seconds, and got back to writing. She had her answer and enjoyed the first really full-bodied rolling of her eyes of the vacation.

Carolyn: This book you're writing is going to be hilarious.

Peter: Could you please try to forget I'm even writing a book?

Carolyn: That will be a lot easier if you would stop writing down what mint your dollar bills came from. Do you have to document everything?

Peter: I don't know what will emerge as the theme yet.

Carolyn: How about, "I never actually saw anything because I was too busy writing down what I saw."

Peter: Wait, let me write that down.

Actually I was glad she came up with the "Mint" line. It reminded me to exchange some dollars for Euros at the airport kiosk. I told her it was good to get at least a little money exchanged now. What if we landed and suddenly needed to buy a Three Musketeers bar? Another eye roll, but she was a little half-hearted about this one because she really likes Three Musketeers bars.

We were in seats 11G and 11H. Each seat had its own entertainment system with movies, TV shows, music, and video games. The flight took seven and a half hours. It took us six hours and forty-five minutes to figure out how to work the video that told us how to use the entertainment system. We ended up getting the picture to work on my screen and the sound to work on Carolyn's armrest.

When I took breaks from smacking the little TV screen, I started writing some ideas for the book. To me the best approach was to base it on things I knew about and to make it funny. I started with the idea of my daughter being in Florence without anybody she knew around. That certainly didn't elicit any chuckle-worthy moments. Obviously I was trying too hard, plus I had too much time. My best work always came right at the deadline. I kept at it, trying to think of an angle, but eventually I fell asleep and started dreaming. I dreamt I was meeting with the literary agent in Venice. In my dream he was an urbane, cultured pearl of a man, with wavy salt and pepper hair, and a permanent tan. He reeked of class, but he couldn't stop laughing at the hilarious manuscript he was reading. Finally, he wiped the tears of mirth from his eyes, let out a few last chortles, plopped the pages down on a table and said, "I'm sorry, but I couldn't put that down, it was hilarious. Only twelve years old and this kid is already the next Woody Allen…okay, so I looked over your stuff. Not my cup of tea. Good luck, though. Now, if you'll excuse me, I'm having lunch with the D'Adamos."

September 9: According to Dino

I actually don't remember much of this day, aside from the fact that I finally understood the meaning of the word "conflicted." I'm looking forward to this great vacation to the land of my ancestors, but I'm also paralyzed by the anticipation of spending two weeks with *the Grecos*. It's starting to overpower any excitement I'm deriving from the trip itself. It's like when I was a little kid unable to sleep on Christmas Eve, except in reverse. My wife, Cathy, actually enjoys the Grecos, so I try to appear as though I'm looking forward to it. It's impossible. It's like being forced to smile while you're having your kidney removed. She doesn't seem to notice, but I know she does. After twenty years of marriage, I'm wise to her little games.

We manage to fly first class to Roma. Somehow the little woman has convinced me that it actually takes fewer frequent flyer miles than if we travel coach. Yeah, OK. I should mention that my wife was born in Taiwan and is half American, half Chinese. Or Taiwanese. Whatever. Bottom line is, she doesn't like white guys, which is why she married me. So she could be sure to do everything within her power to destroy my life. I knew this when I married her, but she's very hot, and I'm Italian, so what are you gonna do? We have three kids. I can't remember their names, but I think they're all boys. They're definitely closer to Cathy than they are to me. The first word each of them spoke was "Mommy." Cathy says that's because they love her more. I just think "white devil" was harder to pronounce.

The flight lasts a little over eight hours. Most guidebooks suggest you take a sleeping pill as soon as you get on board so you can sleep the whole way through and get there refreshed, which is what I would do if I were in coach. But I have free booze and my choice of free movies in first class, so I pocket the pill (intending to slip it into one of the Grecos' drinks, depending on which one of them becomes most annoying first), drink a bottle of wine and

17

two scotch and waters, and watch three movies. By the time we land, not only am I dead tired, but I am also hung over, and my eyes feel like they did when a Jewish ex-girlfriend threw a handful of kosher salt into them. Don't ask.

Wednesday, September 10: Peter's Version

We glided in over the terraced hills on the west coast of Italy, and I was about to wax rhapsodic over the view of the timeless hills and farms when, for the thirtieth time in three days, Carolyn asked if she packed the right clothes. Carolyn was concerned that Cathy's flair and style would make Carolyn look boring by comparison. I told her that boring people don't pack a different pair of shoes for each course at dinner. I also predicted that Dino would wear shorts and sneakers everywhere. Carolyn said Cathy would make him dress nicely. I asked Carolyn if she'd ever met Dino.

We landed a couple of minutes ahead of schedule, and we could tell just by looking at the workers outside the terminal that it was hot and humid in Rome. We already had that up-all-night funk about us, so all I could think about was an air conditioned ride to a hotel with a shower. We got off the plane, and I texted Dino to let him know we had landed. They had gotten in just fifteen minutes ahead of us. We went through immigration, got our bags, and found Cathy and Dino.

They still didn't have all their luggage when we met them, but just when I started to wonder how Dino would make this my fault, the bags showed up and we started looking for the driver who was supposed to take us to the hotel. I asked what we should look for, and Dino said, "An Italian guy with keys." Fortunately, Cathy had a few more details. The transportation area was crowded, and I got my ass pinched about forty times. I was about to ask Cathy to stop or I would tell Dino, but we finally found our driver, Stefano.

We made our way out to Stefano's ultra-mini minivan. It had plenty of room for the four of us, but unfortunately, we also had to squeeze Stefano and our luggage in, so we were crammed pretty tightly. Dino called shotgun, and as we drove, Stefano gave some commentary about the sites. It would have been nice to incorporate Stefano's comments into my notes, but I couldn't hear him over the sound of all four air conditioning vents blasting at Dino's chest.

Stefano might have known a lot about the history of Rome—but he clearly knew nothing about the geography. One end of the street our hotel was on was blocked off, so he took us by another route—through Madrid. It took an hour and ten minutes for him to cover a stretch we covered on foot in about fifteen minutes the next afternoon. And he only got us within a block of the hotel at that: we had to get out and carry our bags the rest of the way. While we were getting out, Dino told me that in Italy it was customary to give the cabbie the finger instead of a tip. But Stefano kept following me around with his hand out while I unloaded the car, so I took his hint instead, thus avoiding a trip to the emergency room. Regrettably, I ignored Dino when he correctly told me that 10 percent was a sufficient tip, so Stefano got 20 percent for making me nauseous and taking thirty-five minutes longer than necessary to get us three-quarters of the way to our destination.

We checked into the Hotel Artorius on Via Del Boschetto. It was on a narrow side street that would have been a little worrisome if half the streets in Rome weren't little side streets. We entered the building and walked down a little hallway to a foyer not much bigger than a living room. To the right was the front desk, really more like a small counter. Behind the counter was a desk with a TV on the wall above it that was on at all times. I swear they watched the same soccer game for five days. In the middle of the foyer was an old elevator with an old-fashioned cage car with cables attached to the top. Suitcases were piled up inside it. As I walked over to it, an employee of the hotel told me, "It's still an elevator, but it's not safe for people anymore, only housekeepers."

There was an atrium past the foyer where they served breakfast in the morning, and wine and pistachios at cocktail hour. The hotel was small, but it had exactly what the four of us wanted: good location, comfort, convenience, spacious rooms, and wine and pistachios in the atrium at cocktail hour. Oh, one other detail: every employee of the place was young and good-looking. There was the good-looking daytime front desk manager, the good-looking housekeeper, the good-looking girl who put out the food for breakfast. The only exception was the old man who sat behind the counter watching the marathon soccer game. Turns out he owned the place. The good-looking daytime front desk guy, Nicolo, gave us a map of the city and some recommendations on restaurants in the area. Our rooms wouldn't be ready for a few hours. Evidently they were going to use the elevator to take our bags upstairs, and that could take a while depending on how many times the elevator crashed and they had to get medical attention for the housekeeper. So we decided to go for a walk, see a few sights, and get the lay of the land.

Via Nazionale is one of the main streets in Rome and runs from the bus and train terminal area all the way across to the Tiber River. It was just a block north of our hotel and there are a number of essential services (banks, pharmacies, ticket offices, etc.) located on this street. Intersecting Via Nazionale are many side streets with interesting little restaurants and shops that are less "touristy." Like any major urban artery, Via Nazionale can be a little difficult to negotiate at first, but we managed to cross and came to the Quirinale. The Quirinale is an official government residence; a beautiful building with impressive columns and architectural flourishes, but the guards, gates, and entrances remind you it is an active, functioning facility, rather than a museum or memorial. From the plaza in front of the Quirinale you can see all the way west to the Vatican. This was our first foray into Rome and we could already tell that almost every turn would reveal a view worth savoring. We took some pictures and then followed some twisting, sloping streets that eventually led to the Trevi Fountain. Built originally in 16 B.C. the fountain was the end point of one of the great Roman aqueducts. There were multiple improvements and enhancements made on the fountain, all the way up to the eighteenth century, before it was finally considered finished. The fountain emerges from an ornate façade that depicts scenes of its mythical origins. And even though the myth included the original designers getting help from a virgin, Dino was underwhelmed and said it was smaller than he thought it would be. We took the obligatory pictures and video clips, and then moved on to find the Spanish Steps on the Piazza di Spagna. That was pretty easy. Our daughter Ali had lived in Spain for a while and mentioned there were Plazas de Espana in Madrid, Seville, and Barcelona. I wonder if the Spanish had some sort of protection racket going on at some point. "Hey, you put up a Plaza de Espana and maybe we won't invade you next week." Who knows, but this plaza was pretty impressive to me. You arrive at a beautiful fountain and beyond are the grand Spanish Steps.

No matter the time of day, there are people moving about, locals and tourists alike, but all contributing to a buzz of activity that has you constantly turning your head. I should point out that tourists are warned to be wary of pickpockets and this being our first day I was especially alert. However I had taken the precaution of leaving our passports in the hotel safe and was using a money belt around my neck under my shirt. With these steps I never felt threatened throughout the trip. I think the money bag was pretty obvious since Carolyn had me put her hairbrush, camera and make-up in it in addition to our cash. I looked like I was sporting a 36D bra filled with digital breasts. I wouldn't be surprised if the pickpockets considered reaching inside my sweaty shirt to get at the money belt and decided to give up crime altogether. Dino said he thought the Spanish Steps were also a little smaller than he had expected. Cathy looked at him sideways and mumbled something about being used to finding things smaller than expected.

We scaled the steps, and at the summit a vendor was selling eight euro bottles of water. I got one. Now you might say it was a mistake to pay that much for a small bottle of water. The real mistake was letting Carolyn drink most of it. That was an error in judgment I would barely live to regret and not make again. From the top we had a great view of one of the high-end shopping districts of downtown Rome. After catching our breath, we walked down the steps and straight ahead up a crowded street. Less than a block away we found the Café Greco. The place had the name "Greco" on the sidewalk, on an awning, and on a plaque outside the front door. We took some pictures, although I don't think Dino took any with his camera. He was looking for a building with the name "D'Adamo" on it. Good luck.

From here we decided to meander back to the hotel. The heat and humidity were starting to get to me. Dino was wearing shorts, and the wives were wearing summer dresses. I was wearing what felt like lead pants and a hair shirt. But I soldiered on without complaint.

If you took an aerial shot of the path we took back to the hotel, it would appear the objective was to get as close to the hotel as possible without actually getting to the front door. We circled it like a freaking bull's-eye, all the while getting more and more exhausted and overheated. The problem was that I hadn't yet figured out that the landmarks on the map were illustrated as if you were facing them at the particular intersection, even though in many cases they were facing a different direction when you actually got there. So I'd look at a cathedral and figure, "I'm facing the front here at the intersection of Prosciutto and Provolone," but I would actually be facing the ass of the damn thing. Another factor was that the streets of Rome were laid out by a dyslexic heroin addict who was sniffing glue and looking through a funhouse mirror when he drew up the plans.

Finally, Dino suggested we walk up a sadistically steep stairway. When I say steep, I mean the locals were rappelling down the handrails. I think I saw snow at the top. A nun was yodeling, for God's sake. But we climbed it, cursing Dino the whole way. I was hoping to have a nice quick stroke and get it out of the way so the other three could enjoy the rest of the vacation. When we got to the top, we were at our street. Dino was right. I was already feeling sick from the heat and now I had to cope with Dino being right on directions, my specialty. I guess at that point Dino decided to quit while he was ahead, because he didn't suggest another turn the rest of the trip.

Right about this time the first germ of an idea for the theme of my book was beginning to emerge – how I died in Italy. Between the heat, lack of sleep, and dehydration I was getting weaker by the minute. I began hallucinating that I wouldn't live to meet with Paul, the literary agent, and with my last ounce of strength I would tell Carolyn to carry on without me and bring him my notes. The book would be called "When I Said I Wanted to See Rome before I Die, It Was a Figure of Speech". It would be published posthumously and the royalties would cover the cost of my daughters' weddings, my grandchildren's education, and Carolyn's upgrade from a Mazda Prelude to a BMW convertible. Just as I was going to ask for a priest to administer last rites, Dino suggested we have something to eat before going back to the hotel to check in. Carolyn and Cathy liked the idea. Thankfully we were just around the corner from a little place off of Via San Milano called, I believe, Diamonte, and shortly after we ordered, I went downstairs to the men's room to write a few last notes and then die on a cool tile floor. It was there that I discovered that Italians have eliminated the "toilet seat down- toilet seat up" debate by taking the toilet seats off altogether in public restrooms.

When I still wasn't dead after two or three minutes I went back up to the table and was going to pass out when my cannelloni appeared. I figured it would be a waste to die before trying at least one taste of authentic Italian food, so I took one bite, then another. Within seconds, my head started to clear. Next I was sending Carolyn a psychic message to let me try her margarita pizza. It worked. Delicious. Dino got eggplant parmigiana, and Cathy got a salad and bread. In what would be a pattern we would see the rest of the trip, Dino got worked up because Carolyn's choice was what he should have ordered. Maybe this *was* going to be a good vacation. I have always maintained that food—especially Italian food, ice cream, and baked goods—has greater healing power than medicine or prayers. It was gratifying to see my faith in fat rewarded.

On the way back to the hotel, I practically bounded down the street. Okay so the dying in Rome idea wasn't going to work out, but on the bright side, I was going to live at least a little longer. We checked into the hotel and went up to our respective rooms, which were very nice. Ours had a big window that looked out on the street, but the big story on Action news was - Dino and Cathy had a balcony. Maybe this balcony was only big enough for a chair and a flower pot, but that didn't diminish Dino's unadulterated joy. In fact the notion that only he could fit on the balcony made it even better. Over the next five nights, we would visit their room for a nightcap. Cathy, Carolyn, and I would sit in the room on chairs or on the bed. Dino would be sitting out on the balcony. He couldn't hear our conversation, which in his eyes only enhanced the experience. Occasionally he would yell in a comment or ask somebody to pour him more wine, but for the most part the balcony was his fortress of solitude. Everybody won.

But back to the first afternoon; digesting the big lunch at Diamonte was beginning to have an effect on all of us and so we repaired to our rooms for a nap. I closed the shutters, turned out the lights, and we crashed. It was a glorious thirty-five minutes of unconsciousness. When I woke up, I was reenergized. I took a shower, got dressed, and headed down to meet Dino for wine and pistachios in the little room off the lobby.

Cathy has worked in the jewelry business for a number of years and generously offers to get good deals on gifts for family and friends. Our trip was scheduled right around my wedding anniversary, so a few months before the trip, I asked Cathy if she could get me a good price on a nice diamond ring. I didn't get Carolyn much of a ring when we got engaged. That was due partly to the fact that I had no money, plus the first time I proposed to a girl she took the ring and still said no, so I wasn't going to break the bank on a hunch. Anyway, with Cathy's help, I was able to get a nicer ring. She brought it with her, and now I just had to figure out when to give it to Carolyn. There were two obvious choices: either the first romantic evening we were alone, or the first time I screwed up and needed a major save. There would be a good number of romantic evenings during the trip, but I screwed up before the sun set on our first day. Electricity did me in.

The layout of the hotel was interesting. An electronic passkey was needed to open the door to your floor, and then a separate, traditional key opened the door to your room. This key was then inserted into a slot on the wall just inside the room. I thought this was to make sure you didn't lose the key, but it turned out that when the key is in the slot, it notifies the maid somebody is in the room. Oh, and one other thing: the electricity doesn't go on unless the key is in the slot.

Dino was already up from his nap, showered, and resplendent in a clean Rutgers University T-shirt and shorts when I arrived in the atrium. He was having a glass of wine, looking at one of the maps, and talking to his new friend, Mario. Mario was the good-looking night-desk manager. He had a sweet disposition and little knowledge of the English language, or anything else for that matter. We kind of expected there would be a few hotel and restaurant employees who didn't speak much English, but it was surprising that this guy who worked the front desk from five until midnight didn't know of any nearby places to eat (three restaurants were within one hundred feet of the front door). When I would ask him a question, he would say in broken English, "OK ... uh ... comeback ... morning and I have it." That was OK when I asked for the closest train station, but he gave the same answer when I asked how late he would be at the desk that night. He also gave the same answer when I asked how old he was and where he lived. Of course, when we would come back for the answer the next morning, he was off duty. Either this guy went home to do exhaustive research, or, as I suspect, he was the handsomest airhead in Western Europe. But he knew where the wine and pistachios were kept, and when we went out at night, he kept our keys so we wouldn't lose them or have them stolen. He didn't once lose the keys...which were kept in a box next to the TV at the front desk. The girls loved him, which didn't surprise me given his looks and ingratiating smile, but Dino's man crush was completely unexpected. We would be out having dinner, and Dino would suddenly blurt out, "Do you think Mario's OK?" Or, "Should we bring back some brascioli for Mario?" Or, "Do you think Mario would like the way this shirt brings out the green of my eyes." At first I chalked it up to the fact that Mario knew where they kept the free wine, but then I found out we were paying for the wine. At that point I decided to walk behind Dino whenever possible.

So we were having wine and pistachios and using *our* map to show Mario how to get to *his* house from the hotel when Dino got a text from Cathy. She asked if I was with him. He replied yes. Then she texted again, asking if I had the room key. I nodded and again, he replied yes. Then she called and said Carolyn needed me upstairs right away. So I ran up the stairs, unlocked the door, and entered the room—the totally dark room. I put my key in the slot, and suddenly there was light, and my furious wife. She explained that when I took the key she couldn't do anything because I essentially took the lights with me. I apologized profusely. And then, as is her wont, Carolyn proceeded to restate my transgression five more times, in subtly different ways each time. I ignorantly pointed out that neither of us knew the thing about the key in the slot for the lights, which prompted yet one more strongly worded review of the events of the previous twenty minutes.

With that I went out and knocked on Cathy's door and told her

I was going to need that ring *tout de suite*. She obliged, and I went back to our room. Carolyn was starting to tell me—again—what she did when she woke up and couldn't turn on the lights, when I said, "Happy anniversary," and gave her the ring. Her jaw dropped, her eyes bugged out, and she called me a son of a bitch, more because I trumped her tirade than anything else. Now I had a very slight upper hand and I told her to hurry up or she would make us late for dinner—before I apologized about the key one more time and let her tell me what I wanted to wear when we went out that night. I realized I had expended all my leverage for the next two weeks, but I calculated, correctly I might add, that merely gesturing toward her finger for the rest of the trip would compensate for any further foul-ups.

I went back downstairs, keyless, and rejoined Dino, who was now showing Mario how to use a fork. Cathy came down shortly thereafter, and finally Carolyn. Earlier Dino had asked the regular manager for a restaurant recommendation, and he gave us the card for a spot called Due Columno, which was just around the corner. It had tables outside and a nice little crowd, so we felt we had a winner. Dino scored pretty well at dinner with veal saltimbocca, Cathy got lasagna, Carolyn and I had penne and linguini carbonara respectively. We shared a pizza with sausage as an appetizer, and the sausage was sweet, very lightly spiced, beautiful. For wine we decided to get a carafe of the house red and went that route for almost every night for two weeks. There must have been five different times when we stopped eating and just looked around and marveled at the thought of finally being in Rome. Dino would punctuate his sighs with a, "Can you fucking believe this?" Of course, I jotted down what everybody ate and endured the reactions: Cathy smiling and tilting her head as if to say, "Isn't that cute, poor little dumbass writing his notes"; Carolyn rolling her eyes to the point she needed a cold compress; and Dino rattling off one-liners about me probably referring to notes during sex. To that point I replied that I needed notes because it's so easy to forget when there is such a long gap between opportunities—a come back that was worth the shot in the ribs from Carolyn. I put up with this abuse and indicated I wanted to have details of the trip in case anybody wanted to refresh their memory some day. Dino said, "Refresh? How about erase?"

After dinner, we lazily walked along the Via Serpenti and came upon a gelateria that we ended up going to almost every night in Rome. I'm a traditional ice cream fan. A generous scoop of 8% milk fat ice cream is about all I need on a warm summer night, or a spring afternoon, or first thing in the morning on Thanksgiving. The only gelato I'd had was at a casino in New Jersey and it didn't really get the job done, but the stuff in Rome was a whole different animal. On this first night, I got dolce de leche in a cone. It was rich and creamy and just sweet enough. They were crazy enough to let us sample as many flavors as we'd like before making a final selection; insanity. When we walked in the next night they immediately put all the sampling spoons away. After gelato, we then walked leisurely around the small side streets. In this part of Rome we felt very safe. In a few minutes, we came to the Piazza del Monti, only a quarter mile from our hotel. People of all ages would hang out there at all hours of the day and night; half of them seemed to be walking dogs. It was full of activity, so I assumed there were people waiting to pick our pockets or steal our wives' purses, but there was never even a close call. Either the thieves weren't there, or it was a tip of the cap to Dino's random shoulder twitching which made it look like he was ready and willing to punch somebody, probably me, but prospective muggers didn't know that…

We got back to the hotel and beat the hell out of a bottle of wine in the D'Adamo suite before heading back to our room. As Carolyn read her way to sleep, I looked over my notes and wrote down some quick ideas to incorporate into the book. Perhaps this was not a good idea after a few solid hours of drinking. The ideas were:

> Lady eats dinner near the Forum, meets a dog, they like ice cream
>
> Guy gets murdered by a chef with a toilet seat
>
> Three guys, no wait one guy, maybe a whole bunch of guys, no that's stupid, good idea. Work on this some more.

When I got up the next morning I must have still been drunk because I crossed off all of the ideas except the last one.

Still, all in all it was a great first day in Rome, especially since I didn't die.

September 10: According to Dino

When we meet up with the Grecos, Peter tells me how they "glided in over the Italian west coast blah, blah, blah, blah, blah." Who's he kidding? For all he knew, he was flying into Newark. I love it when he tries to get poetic and get in touch with his feminine side. Unfortunately, it's his only side. Actually that's not fair, he has two sides. Both feminine.

We meet Pete and Carolyn in the airport, and they're all bubbly and wide awake. I'm bushed, my head's pounding, and I really don't feel like talking so when Pete asks me who we're looking for I can't stop the normal D'Adamo sarcastic response. Pete says that, unlike everyone else, I lack an internal editor in my head, and that anything that pops into my brain is immediately transformed into words. According to Pete, the only modification is the addition of numerous four-letter words. He's wrong of course. I don't add them. They're actually part of the cognitive process. I even think in curses. To be honest, when I hear some people curse, I cringe because it sounds so bad. I just happen to be very good at it. In my case, the cursing merely provides an interesting backdrop of color commentary and, oddly enough, is never offensive. It's just a talent I have. A gift really. Like the ability to bring out the worst in people.

Getting back to the story, I'm tired and I don't feel like talking, so when Pete asks me what the driver looks like, I say, "An Italian guy with keys." Now, anybody but Pete would get the point and just let it go, but not Pete. He's very concerned that we might never find the guy and that we might have to spend the next two weeks at the airport. Then he starts bitching because he's getting his ass pinched. If you ever saw Pete's ass, you'd know that his ass getting pinched twenty times is the same as a normal sized ass getting pinched once. So even though we already have all our luggage, I make believe we have another piece and I have to go find it because I can't seem to spot it on the conveyor belt. I find the nearest bar and order *due sorso di* (two shots of) grappa. I soon discover that drinking sufficient amounts of grappa dulls my senses, which makes certain aspects of the trip much easier to endure.

Anyway, sure enough, we spy an Italian guy with keys, and it's Stefano, our driver. I can immediately tell that he has that "Italian" way about him. In America, when you meet a guy you are *paying*, he greets you with a smile and is very gracious. In Italy, he acts like you're his unemployed brother-in-law who his wife made him pick up and will be sleeping on his sofa for the next two weeks.

We pass the Monumente Nazionale a Vittorio Emanuele three times, and unless there are three of them, I'm guessing that we're lost. Stefano probably forgot that we were paying him a flat fee. When he remembers, he just stops the car right in the middle of the road and tells us the hotel is two blocks in that direction. That's OK with me, I was getting carsick anyway. So I grab my luggage and let Stefano know how much I enjoyed the ride by giving him the appropriate American hand gesture. Pete tells the girls that I told him to give Stefano the finger because it's a compliment in Italy. To set the record straight, I tell them I didn't tell him to give Stefano the finger. In Italy it doesn't mean anything. I told Pete to give him the American "OK" hand sign, which in Italy means, "Up your ass." Instead Pete gives him the finger anyway, so it isn't funny. It's like when I'm drinking with Pete at a bar in Venice toward the end of the trip and I tell him that there's a customary toast, "Offro io," but you have to say it loudly. It actually means, "This round is on me," but Pete doesn't pronounce it right, so he just sounds like a drunken American (which, ironically, is exactly what he was, but once again, not funny). Carolyn, on the other hand, is much more accommodating. At the end of a meal one night, I tell her that the way to tell the waiter she loved the food is to say, "Voglio fare lamore con te." Obviously, what the waiter heard was that she wanted to go to bed with him. Priceless. I could always count on Carolyn.

It's ungodly hot, and about halfway to the hotel I turn around and say to Cathy, "Hey, nice job finding Stefano." She gives me one of her "looks," drops the bag she's lugging, and responds via—you guessed it—hand gesture, in this case the appropriate one. Did I mention that she has a problem with white guys?

When we arrive at the hotel we aren't able to check in yet so we drop off the luggage and decide to take a walk to see the Trevi Fountain and the Spanish Steps, which we're told aren't far away. When we get there, I say they look a lot smaller than I thought they'd be. Carolyn says that's what Cathy said, and they all start laughing. I am ready for an appropriate comeback but decide that their comment is too juvenile and any retort would be beneath me. We still want to kill some time and get a feel for the area, but soon it's clear that we're walking around in circles, as Pete is getting us lost left and right (*sinistra e destra*). He's starting to actually make Stefano look good, when I finally have to step in and take charge ... again. I tell him that he's screwing up because all the landmarks on the map are facing the same way but that in reality they point in different directions. Pete looks at me like I'm crazy (*pazzo*), and says, "Why would they make the maps wrong?" I tell him that this is Italy, and it's just one more opportunity to bust our balls. Evidently this explanation makes sense to him, and within five minutes we're almost back at the hotel. During those five minutes he takes exceptional pleasure in pointing out all the things we pass that are named Greco. Big deal. It's like he's proud that his last name is the Italian equivalent of Jones. I let it go because in Italian, "Greco" means "Greek." Poor guy doesn't know what the hell he is.

At this point, since we're now so close to the hotel, we decide to stop for lunch. I can't remember what everyone eats except for Carolyn, who orders pizza. I do remember that everything is very good, and we all rave about our first real Italian meal, except for Carolyn, who isn't saying much. Now, when you brag about your meal, good manners dictate that you let others taste it. So we're all thinking that Carolyn's not enjoying her pizza. But she eats the whole thing except for one little slice and then finally says, nonchalantly, "Does anyone want this?" We all decide to take a little bite, and it is the best damn pizza we have ever tasted. That little shit. I make a mental note to never trust her again.

We get to the hotel, and although it's late afternoon, we take a little nap, a custom I absolutely love. Afterwards, I get ready before everyone else and head down to the lobby, where Mario, the guy at the desk greets me. "Dino! Come stai?"

"Molto bene, Mario," I respond. "Avete un vino di rosso?"

"Certo," Mario says. "I have a nice red wine for you. Have a seat."

I take a seat in the little courtyard that is between the hotel and another building. It's a wonderful little space where grape vines have grown overhead providing a natural canopy. It's blissfully quiet, and you get the feeling like you're in ... well, Italy. Mario brings me a full glass of red wine and leaves the bottle, which has another half glass left in it. He says, "There's a little left ina da bottle, Dino. Why not?" I'm not sure if that means I'm paying for it or not, but I don't care, I'm in heaven. All alone. Not a Greco or Asian in sight. Mario brings me pistachio nuts and a plate full of little wafers. If I was gay, I'd marry that son of a bitch. I play Dean Martin songs on my iPhone and slowly sip from my *bicchieri di vino*. I'm thinking it just doesn't get any better than this, and then, a little later, it does. When people ask me what my favorite part of Italy was, I say, "Dinner." I'm telling you, the food in every town and every city we visit was beyond belief.

Peter comes down first, with a look on his face like he just got lucky. Either that or he just went to the bathroom. I can't tell. But he does look happy. I'm in such a good mood that I'm actually glad to see him and turn up the iPhone. Petey joins me in a glass. We don't say a thing. It's magical in that little courtyard, and of course, there's Mario. When the girls come down we walk for about a block and sit outside a place that looks like an upscale pizza parlor called Due Columno. The waiter is a real character, like a guy you'd find back in Jersey. He and I keep kibitzing back and forth in Italian and English throughout dinner. Finally, he asks me how I liked my meal, and I tell him, "E schivo, ma meglio della Cucina di mia moglie." He laughs out loud because I said that it sucked but it was better than anything my wife ever cooked. He then puts an entire bottle of grappa on our table, and so continues my love affair with Italy's version of grain alcohol. Pete and I drink till our eyelids get stiff, and it takes us fifteen minutes before we're both able to stand up at the same time. The waiter gets a good tip, and I leave shaking my finger at him and calling him names in Italian that I don't know the meaning of but remember hearing as a kid working construction with my father in Elizabeth, New Jersey. He's laughing and tells us in Italian to make sure we come back tomorrow night. Either that or to get the hell out and never come back again. I am pretty drunk (*umbriago*) and not sure what he says, but as they say in Italy, *e lo stesso* (who cares)?

Everyone then goes for gelato. We never rely on guidebooks to find things since it is always better to just ask the locals where the best "whatever" is, and it usually works out great. We ask someone we pass on the street, and they tell us to go to a place a few blocks away. The short walk in the night air clears our heads a bit and is definitely worth the effort because the gelato shop is fantastic. Long glass display cases with at least thirty different flavored gelatos, each screaming, "picka me, picka me." They gave you a taste (*assaggiare*) of any flavor you want, and everyone has a tough time ruling anything out. I would normally forego the gelato, thinking that I'd make up for it by drinking more grappa later, but tonight I decide on a chocolate, pistachio, espresso concoction. Or maybe it was the cappuccino, amaretto combo. I can't remember, but I do remember loving whatever the hell it was. There is nothing like walking while eating gelato. You don't really care where you are heading as long as your spoon keeps coming up from that little paper cup with more gelato in it. We eventually find ourselves in a little square with the obligatory ancient stone fountain in its center which is surrounded by more restaurants and a couple of shops that are still open despite the late hour. Almost midnight and there are plenty of locals still milling about, mostly young people.

I think it is really cool to see how the Italians live. Eat late, stay up late, have some gelato in the wee hours and just kick back. The only drunks I see on the whole trip are tourists, including us. They are obnoxious. We are funny.

We hung with the young Italians for a while listening to someone strum a guitar against the backdrop of the equally melodic sound of soft Italian chatter. Then back to the hotel. Said good night. Hit the sack. Had a nightmare about the Grecos ... again.

Wednesday, September 11: Peter's Version

Carolyn and I overslept a little. By the time we came downstairs for breakfast, there wasn't much food left at the little buffet, and Dino and Cathy were ready to go. Dino and I have the same posture in a chair when we want to get moving. You move the chair away from the table a little bit. You straighten one leg out in front of you, put one hand in your pocket, and play with whatever you've got in the pocket. The other hand is on the table tapping. The other leg is busy with the heel tapping—at a rate of about sixty taps per second. There are drum rolls slower than this tapping. I saw Dino in this posture and figured it was time to move out. Carolyn saw this and said, "How long would it take to make an espresso?" Actually, we were kind of eager to get started ourselves, so we just gulped down some orange juice, grabbed a croissant, and headed out. The juice was from blood oranges so it was darker and richer tasting, but not as tangy as the fresh squeezed Valencia orange juice we get in the states. It was delicious. I asked how breakfast was. Dino said it was pretty nice. Pretty nice to Dino means good but not nearly heavy enough. That would be just right for me so I decided to be sure I got up in time for breakfast for the rest of the trip.

The hotel Cathy found was in an ideal spot, just a few blocks north of some of the greatest historical sites in all of Rome. According to the map, it was a short walk to the Colosseum; straight line right down via Serpenti, which changes names at Via Cavour. Almost every road in Rome changes names at some point. I think the Chamber of Commerce does this so you will wander through the city and stop at shops and restaurants to ask for directions, and then out of guilt buy something. Fortunately, although this road changed names a couple of times, it did not change direction, so in less than ten minutes we were eye to eye with the fourth floor of the Colosseum. Being eye to eye with the fourth floor means you are about thirty-five feet above the entrance level, and it took us three or four attempts to find the right path to where we get in. Had we looked at the map first, we might have cut that down to two or three attempts. Across the street from the Colosseum was a tourist center/convenience store that sold a package that included free admission to the Colosseum and one other museum, a discount off other sites, and a three-day bus pass … or we could trade it all for what was behind the curtain. So far, everything Cathy had suggested worked great, so we bought four of the packages and headed for the Colosseum.

Even though we could see it from three blocks away, it was hard to appreciate just how big the Colosseum is. I'll try to express it as lyrically as I can. The Coliseum is big. It is also old. The guidebooks tell us the Colosseum was used for all kinds of epic Roman events, and that's probably true. We walked through all the concourses where they must have had the concession stands for food and pennants and gladiator trading cards. Now these areas just have artifacts. You look at the sheer size and detail of the Colosseum, and you marvel at how they did it. Think about it: no television contract, nobody paying for naming rights. How did they afford this thing?

We wandered through the Colosseum in awe of its scale. Walking through the covered areas was fairly comfortable, but out in the sun it was oppressively hot. Dino took some video of me sweating; real cinema verite. The stone walkways are over two thousand years old and very uneven. You don't read much about gladiators tripping on their way to gladiate, so maybe these things just settled over time and people get a thrill walking where the Romans walked—until they go down in a heap trying to find a hot dog stand. We were lucky Cathy's bad back didn't get aggravated. We were in the Colosseum for about twenty minutes when Dino looked at me and said, "Yeah, it's very impressive, I guess, but it doesn't *do* anything. No fireworks, no light show, no simulated lions attacking simulated Christians. Obviously the people who run this place never consulted with anybody from Disney or Vegas." How do you respond to that?

In the package we bought was a map of the Colosseum area, which includes the Forum, but I'll be damned if I could figure out which was *the* Forum. The first place we thought was the Forum turned out to be where Caesar kept chickens. Then we went to a place that used to be a hall for entertaining but is now a yard with some stones on it. Then we came to a building called a forum, but it wasn't Caesar's Forum, it was somebody else's. Amazingly, a large number of buildings used for everyday functions are still in remarkably good condition for being over 2000 years old. I couldn't help thinking that if structures like this existed back home that they would be converted into real estate offices.

The Hippodrome, used as an athletic and entertainment venue was of a scale that would accommodate a lot of professional events even today, but what knocked Dino out was the Arch of Titus. I didn't mention to him that this giant arch doesn't actually have any function except to brag on Emperor Titus. I mean it's big, but you could walk around it just as easily as walk under it so it's not like it was a gate to keep people in or out. Maybe they had a thirty-foot-wide turnstile underneath it and you had to go through that to get into Titus's Forum. When you think about the tools and technology that were available then, it is amazing to contemplate that these buildings were even thought of, let alone built. As we walked around we noticed that, by and large, people were pretty respectful and quiet while touring the area. It might have been because everybody was busy trying not to faint in the heat of the day, but I prefer to think it was because they were as taken by the spectacle of ancient Rome as we were.

When we finished with the ruins, we decided to catch a bus to the Pantheon. On the map it looked like it was only a mile or so away, but it was getting *really* hot, and the girls' feet were getting sore. Being an American tourist, I assumed all the buses stopping at the Colosseum would be tour buses, because isn't that why everything is there? Wrong! The bus I chose for us was the equivalent of the "2" bus that takes you from South Philadelphia to Fishtown, neither of which caters to tourists. We were heading in the opposite direction of where we needed to go. Dino was the first to suspect this wasn't the bus we wanted, and he decided to ask the driver how we could get back to the Colosseum. I thought we should ask how we could get to the Pantheon, since that's where we wanted to go. Why not ask if the Pantheon is on this route?

At this point I remind you that Dino said he would handle the language, but we now realized that most of the Italians didn't recognize any of the thirty regular words Dino had learned, however they did seem to fully understand each of the fifty-seven obscenities he also learned. Everybody in Italy knew Dino was cursing at them, they just couldn't figure out why. Nevertheless, I let him handle the negotiations with the bus driver. Dino's strategy seemed to be to simply keep asking the same question over and over again, saying it louder and adding a new gesture every time. Eventually he succeeded in getting us thrown off the bus, along with another passenger who seemed to be trying to get in the middle of the argument. Fortunately, the passenger really did understand what we were trying to do, and he told us where to wait for a bus that would take us back to the Colosseum. I chalked up the whole experience as one of those little fun adventures that we would laugh about later. Dino looked at Cathy and said, "*This* is what I was talking about for the last three months!" When we got back to the Colosseum, we figured that since we had enjoyed fifteen minutes of air conditioning on the bus we were sufficiently refreshed to walk to the Pantheon.

So we hoofed it, and on the way our wives decided to stop and dip their feet in one of the fountains at the Vittorio Emanuele Monument, which is a complex of statues, fountains, and a museum celebrating the unification of Italy in the late 19th century. The museum is made of bright white marble and stands out dramatically from the older darker buildings throughout the city. Unfortunately, Dino and I had walked completely around and about a quarter of a mile away from the monument before we realized Cathy and Carolyn were no longer with us. We figured it out when we passed a shoe store and instinctively stopped so they could look in the window. When we turned around to complain, they weren't there. So we trudged back to the memorial, figuring there must be a guy selling shoes from a cart or something and found them obliviously sitting on the ledge of a fountain chatting away with their feet casually stirring the water. We had passed this monument about eleven times when we were lost the day before, but now I was getting a better idea of the maps and directions. We started up again, stopped at the aforementioned store again, and got to the Pantheon without any trouble, except that we came up behind it.

From behind, the Pantheon looks like the back of a big Knights of Columbus building. Stupid map. But when we got to the front, we were completely taken aback. This building was finished in the first half of the second century. We had to keep reminding ourselves of that. The exterior is reminiscent of many older Greek buildings. In fact "pantheon" is derived from Greek meaning "all gods" as a tribute to all of the gods in early Roman religion. Later it was converted into a Catholic Church. Once you walk inside you notice the elegant, rectangular, earth tone designs in the marble floors, and then your eyes are pulled straight up, over 130 feet, to the dome. Almost all of the light in the Pantheon comes from the single oculus at the peak of the dome. I'm not sure modern architects with industrial tools could duplicate the Pantheon's simple majesty. This is where the remains of Raphael are kept. I didn't mention this because Dino would have been disappointed when I told him I was talking about the artist and not the teenage mutant ninja turtle. Think about the tools that were used 1900 years ago. The circular saws and cement mixers must have run on batteries back then because I didn't see any outlets.

Now we were hungry. We walked around and found a restaurant that wasn't crowded. It turned out there was a reason for that. It was a tourist trap, and we should have been wise to it. It was fancy on the outside and inside, and it was far too close to the Pantheon, but our judgment was clouded by our hunger. There was a special that featured gnocchi and veal. Dino, Cathy, and I got that, and Carolyn got the eggplant. The gnocchi and veal? Not so great, but the eggplant was excellent. Dino, of course, was irked. How come the eggplant was only OK yesterday when he ordered it? Now Carolyn got it, and it was great.

As we walked back to the hotel along a curved street, I noticed a plaque that identified the building as a famous fencing academy founded by Aurelius Greco. I figured Dino would be interested to hear about this, but I was wrong. He was actually a little disappointed. That was a bunch of things named "Greco" in twenty-four hours, and nothing named "D'Adamo." To make him feel a little better, I told him I had seen another building that featured Cathy's maiden name, Kuczmarski. Dino wasn't amused by this tidbit of information either. But this made me think of another book angle. It's a story about a guy who goes back to Italy to trace his roots. His parents never talked about their heritage much; they were focused on being

Americans. After they pass away, he decides to travel all over Italy looking for clues to his family's past. He sees little things that remind him of his Italian grandfather, like seeing an old man negotiating the price of fruit at a stand, or running back to his house because he realized he left home without his pants…again. I rolled this idea around in my head as we walked through the streets of Rome. This could be pretty funny. I decided to call my older brother later in the evening and ask what he remembers of our grandparents just to get some frame of reference.

Having spent a large part of the previous day lost in this section of the city, north and west of the Forum, we were confident we could find our way to the hotel so we took a couple of detours on the way back. There was a beautiful restaurant where they were preparing some sort of elaborate dinner party, and we walked past some of the larger department stores in downtown Rome. (That may be the only time you read "walked past" and "stores" in the same sentence in this entire journal.)

Our walking pattern was pretty predictable. We would start with Carolyn and me in front, with me looking at the map. After about a block, one of us would stop to point something out. It took Carolyn and Cathy about five minutes to look at everything. It took Dino and me about thirty seconds. So the formation would soon change, with Dino and me walking in front, and Carolyn and Cathy trailing us. When we got about a half block ahead of them we would stop, look back, look at each other, roll our eyes, and then stare back at them really hard, thinking that would draw their attention. If it worked we would then make one of three "C'mon, let's go" gestures. One was the tilt of the head in the forward direction. Two involved moving the head forward and opening up the palms as if to say, "What in the world are you doing?" And number three was to slump our shoulders and look down in resignation. Dino didn't do that one too much. Before long, Cathy would see something in a store, get Dino's attention (more on that process later), and Dino would drop back to see what she saw. Then we would resume walking with Carolyn and me in front, but that would never last longer than two blocks before we saw something Dino wanted to photograph, or I saw something I wanted to eat, or Carolyn saw something that would look great in our house.

All in all, it would take us about forty-five minutes to cover a half mile, but I enjoyed every minute of it. It was interesting to note that while there were a lot of things that are commonplace in America, there were a lot of things you would never find in the US. For example, on the day we arrived, everywhere we went we saw calendars for sale that featured strikingly handsome young men dressed as priests. I think we were supposed to believe they really were priests, but I'm not buying it. Cathy or Carolyn would spot these calendars at a stand and just casually say, "Hey, look, there are those calendars again." Then they would slooooowwwlllllyy walk past, staring at the pictures, maybe even lazily turning the page of one if it was open to check out Father August. Then they would hum or sigh. When Cathy would look at them, she would giggle and shake her head. Carolyn would look at them, then at me, then back at the calendar. Then she would look at me and say, "Fix your hair. Don't you have a nicer shirt than that?"

Eventually we made it back to the hotel. It was 5 p.m. and we decided to meet in the lobby at about 6:30. It was nice to relax and get freshened up before going out to dinner. At about 6, I went for a walk by myself around the neighborhood of the hotel and found a market where I bought some wine and snacks to have in the room. At the local stores, a bottle of wine can be pretty reasonable, and the variety of fresh fruit and cheese is excellent considering how small the markets are. I've never lived full time in a city, but I began to imagine that I could pull it off in a city like Rome. The pace was …there was no pace. You did what you had to do and then you bought a little bread and a little cheese and a little wine. Maybe Carolyn would think about a long term move if I could get transferred over here. Okay, I was getting a little ahead of myself, but I really liked the lifestyle.

After wandering around the streets for a few more minutes, I came back, put everything in the room, *left the key*, and met Dino in the atrium for a glass of wine. A little while later, Cathy came down. We waited a few minutes, and then Dino gave Carolyn her new nickname, "Where's Carolyn?" as in, "Pete, is 'Where's Carolyn' going to be down soon or should I go have dinner and come back and have dinner again when she's ready?" On this topic Dino and I were in agreement. 'Where's Carolyn' was the perfect nickname.

I went upstairs to find "Where's Carolyn" putting the last thirty or forty finishing touches on her outfit, before changing her mind and going with something entirely different. We went downstairs, and although Dino was in heel-tap mode, he was well under control. We had no real plan for dinner and just headed out. About a block or so away was a place with outdoor seating called Café Jubilao. A waiter outside was trying to shame passersby into having dinner there. We walked past and told him that we were going to walk up the block and that if we didn't see anything better, we would be back for dinner.

As luck would have it, we were walking the only block in Rome with only one restaurant on it, and the smell of this place called us back. We sat outside. I had a pizza and beer, and the rest of the group had lighter meals after the big, disappointing lunch. There was a guy walking from table to table playing guitar. Strolling troubadours are not Dino's thing. Piped in Dean Martin, Frank Sinatra, and Tony Bennett music are acceptable, Italian folk songs are not. As the minstrel got within ten or fifteen feet of us, he looked at Dino. Dino looked the guy right in the eye, smiled, and nodded as if to say, "You're not getting a tip, and if you come over here and look at our wives, I'll kill you." The guy put down the guitar and ran away. The waiter kept coming over trying to kid around with Dino, or maybe at Dino, and we all tired of it. It's OK to make fun of American tourists, but you'd better be funny. This guy wasn't funny. We finished dinner and decided to just pay and leave instead of lingering over cappuccino. The waiter came over and told us to come back again before we left the city. Dino laughed and said, nah, it wasn't that good. The waiter didn't seem phased.

We walked over to our gelato place and then absentmindedly cruised the neighborhood a little more. Suddenly, upon turning a corner, we found ourselves right back at the Café Jubilao, with the waiter still trying to get a rise out of Dino. We froze and spotted an Irish bar near us and pointed to the door, as if we finally found the place we were looking for… fifteen yards from where we ate dinner an hour ago. We went into the bar, which was called Irish Bar, thinking it would be a neat experience to drink in an Irish bar in Rome. There are bars in unfinished basements in Northeast Philadelphia with twice the charm and half the spores, mold, and fungus of this place. We asked the bartender/owner how he came to own a bar in Rome. Above the noise level of the music it was hard to hear, but I think he said he came for vacation, lost his pants, traded his ticket for a pair of khakis and the lease, and the rest is history.

After a quick drink, we left the bar and made sure not to make eye contact with the Jubilao waiter, which was hard because he was *still* yelling at us from right across the street. If Dino's Italian was really that good he might have been able to figure out what it was about us that got this guy so provoked. I kept checking my pockets to make sure I didn't leave my wallet at the table. Maybe he was yelling that he poisoned the food and had the antidote all ready. We'll never know. When we got back to the hotel, I realized that all night we'd never gotten more then three blocks from the place. We sat near the D'Adamo balcony, drank wine, and talked politics and movies. Of all the potential problems this trip held, none was as fraught with peril as the prospect of a political discussion. You see, Dino thinks Hilary Clinton is the devil—not figuratively, literally. On the other hand, I don't think Dick Cheney casts a reflection in a mirror. In point of fact, Dino and I probably agree on more political topics than we disagree on. But the things we agree on are things like the fact that Franklin Delano Roosevelt had a hitch in his git along. Here's how the political debate went this night:

Dino: "Petey, are you willing to pay ten thousand dollars to see Obama win the election, because that's what it's going to cost you in taxes every year."

Petey: "Sure, Dino, if giving up more of my income will make life better for others, then so be it."

Dino: "But Petey that makes you an asshole."

Petey: "An asshole that's going to heaven."

Dino: "I don't think so, Petey. I don't think anybody that stupid gets into heaven."

44

Petey: "Forget it, Dino. I'm voting for Obama, and I'm going to tell all my friends."

Dino: "You just did."

When we got back to our room I was so worked up from the political debate I couldn't see straight, which is the perfect condition to be in when I talk to my brother, DJ. DJ is like Jesus, he loves everybody, even Dino. I called DJ to ask about our parents and grandparents and our Italian heritage. Being a few years older than me I thought he might have more memories and facts that would guide me through the story idea. The conversation was brief

DJ – Hey, buddy, having a good time over there?

Peter – Yes, it's fabulous

DJ – How's Dino?

Peter – The food is great

DJ – I hear you, what can I do for you?

Peter – I'm trying to write a book using this trip to Italy as the backdrop and one of the ideas I have is to trace our Italian roots, but I really don't know much about our Italian ancestors to get this off the ground. Do you know much about that?

DJ – Uh…what are your other ideas?

Peter – What do you mean?

DJ – Well, Pop Greco came over here to get out of the Italian army. Mom Mom Greco was actually first generation Irish American.

Peter – What about mom's parents?

DJ – Part English, part Scotch, part Saint Bernard

Peter – That explains why Grand pop always had that flask…

DJ – Yep, sorry pal, time for plan B.

Okay, so this might not be the idea I was looking for. I looked at the ideas I drunkenly wrote down the night before one last time before tearing that embarrassing page out of the book. Still, it was only the first full day and it had been a great day overall. And earlier in the day I had that idea of moving to Italy. That could be something to explore. I was still confident that I could put together a compelling outline in time for Venice. As I nodded off to sleep I half dreamed/half imagined Dino looking over my shoulder as I typed telling me he couldn't read the pages but was sure whatever I was typing sucked.

September 11: According to Dino

I snuck a peek at the notebook Pete's been writing in every five minutes and immediately decided that I won't do it again. I don't know what trip he is on but evidently he has reverted to the college versions where hallucinogenic substances are involved. Some people have a problem getting the facts straight but Pete is taking this to a new level, especially when it comes to his comments regarding me. I think he's so used to distorting things that it's become second nature and he actually starts to believe them. I'm sure that's how he handles his memories of high school. In Petey-Land he was probably captain of the football team and homecoming king. Now to be fair, if I had experienced the kind of trauma this poor guy probably did, I'd invent a fantasy world too, but in this case his ramblings are putting yours truly in a bad light, and that crosses the line. OK, got that off my chest, back to the trip …

I have breakfast downstairs. Not the IHOP version of breakfast that I'm used to. This one is lunchmeat on a platter, foil wrapped cheese things, Italian cookie wafer things, cappuccino with the froth in the shape of a heart (I didn't know Mario worked mornings, too). Eventually the Grecos come down, and I surprise myself at how patient I am. Normally I hate waiting for people, but I'm almost calm (not on a normal person calm meter, but I gotta say, it was pretty damn calm for a D'Adamo).

The best thing about our foursome is we're all pretty open about what each of us wants to do, which makes things a lot easier. So today we decide we are going to hit the Colosseum and the Forum, which is easy to do since they are right next to each other. Pete is still navigating, but I'm feeling pretty confident about his ability to get us there for two reasons. One, he's now on to the Italian map trickery. Two, we can see the Colosseum from where we're standing. So we get there with no problem, and it's really incredible to see this huge ancient answer to a modern football stadium (except in this case the Lions actually won once in a while). It was and still is an astounding place. In the old days, the Romans flooded the entire interior of the structure through underground viaducts and actually staged naval battles. Try that at Giants Stadium! You can see the ruins of the lower level where they would open hidden trap doors to surprise unsuspecting gladiators with hungry Bengal tigers (no, not the NFL type, the other kind, who, unlike my wife, actually did like white guys ... a lot). Nice to know that the ancient Romans had a good sense of humor. The history of the Colosseum is mind boggling on so many levels. None of these facts, by the way, are volunteered by Pete, whose job it is to know the history. I learned it by watching the Discovery Channel three months *after* the trip.

I'm also astonished at the brick and stonework used in the construction throughout the Colosseum. Stone masons like my dad laid these stones and bricks thousands of years ago. You could see how they used shells in the concrete mortar to give it more strength. But the most amazing thing about the Colosseum is the simple fact that this huge ancient ruin sits right in the middle of a modern city. I love the U.S., but not even New York City has anything like this. In America, the oldest standing structures might date back to the sixteen hundreds and those are one room log cabins. In Italy, they have shoe stores older than that.

After leaving the Colosseum, Pete becomes obsessed with finding the Forum. The whole damn thing next to the Colosseum is the Forum. He refuses to grasp that simple concept. It's getting embarrassing. He keeps looking at each ruin within the Forum wondering which one is the Forum. It's like a guy sitting in the Bronx watching a Yankees game asking the guy next to him where Yankee Stadium is.

All around us we see Corinthian columns that still stand but now support nothing but air and the remnants of other Roman structures that continue to endure like ancient ghosts. By eavesdropping on a few tour guides, I find out what some of the ruins originally were. Not sure why, but I am a little surprised when I hear that food stalls and brothels were within spitting distance of the Roman Senate. Not so different from Washington,

D.C., I suppose. One particular ruin is identified as the House of the Vestal Virgins. I just can't hear those words without thinking of Procol Harum's song *A Whiter Shade of Pale* and I can't help but visualize a young hottie in a toga with a suitcase waiting for a train that's headed for the coast. Which coast, I have no idea. The Virgins, I learn, were actually a highly honored cult of very attractive Roman women who had a few ceremonial duties and had to keep the sacred flame lit. They had to remain celibate for thirty years at which time they could either retire and get married or they could stay. It sounded like a pretty good gig and I'm sure that despite the rules, there were some wild goings on at the VV Sorority House.

My favorite ruin however, is the Arch of Titus. It is huge, mostly intact and well preserved, and the detailed carvings on the underside of the arch are still in great condition. I'm able to take some very artistic looking photos, but it is hot as hell and after an hour or so of exploring the Forum, I'm ready to pack it in. I'm considering mugging a Japanese tourist that has strayed from the Asian pack and taking her umbrella when Cathy finds me and tells me we're leaving.

On the way out, we decide that since it's still early we will head over to the Pantheon. We have no idea where the Pantheon is, but that doesn't stop Peter from jumping on the first bus he sees across the street. Carolyn, Cathy, and I follow him, and I have to admit, I am slightly impressed. That ends ten seconds later when I ask Pete how he knows this is the right bus. He says he has no idea, but it is a bus, and this is Rome, so it must take us close to the Pantheon sooner or later. I sigh deeply, something I learned to do often when talking with either of the Grecos, and go to talk with the bus driver. In America, you're not supposed to talk to bus drivers. In Italy, you're not supposed to answer them. Now I know why. I figure there's no way we'll get to the Pantheon since this bus is heading in the opposite direction, and the best I can hope for is if it loops back to where it came from so I ask, "Scuzi, ma quale ferme e Colosseum?" Not sure if I said it exactly right but he should get the picture. He gives me the same empty gaze my wife does when I ask her if she wants to fool around. I try saying "Colosseum" ten different ways, all with Italian accents. I use Italian hand gestures. I shrug my shoulders. I do my best Marlon Brando impression and pat him on his chubby, bus-driver cheeks. Nothing helps until finally, one passenger says, "Colloseo"? I nod, and the collective light bulb evidently goes on for every Italian in the first three rows. They all nod in unison and begin jabbering about what an idiot the American is, and why couldn't he just say that in the first place? (I have a similar experience when I ask someone if they have cannoli, but that's another story.) When we get to the next stop (*ferme*), the "helpful" Italian guy (not to be confused with every other Italian on the bus) gets off the bus with us and shows us where to catch the correct bus that will take us back to where we started, since this one obviously never will.

So, finally, we get back to the Colosseum and decide that the safest thing will be to just walk to the Pantheon. It's not too far and on the way there we pass a continuous stream of makeshift parks that are the result of Italians digging for a subway or something and continuously stumbling upon ancient artifacts. At one spot we see a photo of the result of an excavation that recently took place there. In the picture is a beautiful, two-thousand-year-old stone head of a Roman emperor that is well preserved and the size of a Volkswagen. I can imagine how big the rest of him is, still buried in the ground. The Italians just can't stick a shovel in the dirt without hitting something ancient, so they aren't able to get much accomplished. At least that's their excuse. Hey, at least they have an excuse. Back home we're not much better, but not because we discover anything. It's because our public-works projects usually consist of thirty-nine guys leaning against their shovels while the only woman, who looks like the toughest of the bunch, directs traffic.

Because we keep taking wrong turns it takes us about forty minutes, but we finally make it to the Pantheon. Cathy keeps telling me that we can't be going to the Pantheon because the

Pantheon is in Greece, and my lovely wife has never, in twenty years of marriage, ever admitted she was wrong. So when we get to the Pantheon, I finally get to tell her that it's the Parthenon that is in Greece, and that the incredible building we're standing in front of is in fact, the Pantheon. She gives me a look like I just farted in front of the nuns who were walking by (which ironically I actually did, but how the hell did she know?). The astonishing thing about the Pantheon (not the Parthenon) is that it's about as old as the Colosseum but it looks brand new. And it's perfect. The architecture and craftsmanship are truly astounding. All the columns are identical, but they obviously had to have been made by hand. It makes you marvel at how they could have made things so exact without power tools. The huge, ornate ceiling is a dome that even today is considered an engineering marvel. It supports itself by using varying thicknesses of concrete at exact specifications the higher the elevation. Incredible. Once again, information source score: Discovery Channel, 2; Pete Greco, 0.

Friday, September 12: Peter's Version

Today it was Dino and Cathy's turn to sleep in a little bit. I figure he was probably trying to compete with me; proving he could get up earlier than me if he wanted and sleep later if he wanted. Yippee for him! Carolyn and I got to breakfast first. I had an upset stomach, which is not uncommon for me. I have my Mom's stomach. I worry about things that are out of my control and can't possibly happen, and by the way have little in the way of a downside. For example, if I have to catch an early flight, my stomach will be tied up in knots worrying about getting to the airport on time, even though I leave four hours early and there are flights to my destination every hour. Every place we go I plot out the rest room on the way, and failing that, densely wooded areas. It's all part of the charm of being me. After a cup of tea we made our way over to a bank to exchange some dollars for Euros, and when we got back, Dino and Cathy were ready to go. We had decided the night before to go to the Villa Borghese, a huge estate right off of the famed Via Veneto. The villa features a museum, a zoo, formal gardens, and a few other interesting buildings. According to my map it was about a mile and a half away. We decided we would walk.

It was a little overcast and misty all day, but we managed to stay dry and found our way pretty easily. Along the way, Dino took video clips or snapshots of everything from nuns to hot girls on motorbikes. Now if he could have gotten one of the nuns to get on a motorcycle with one of the hot girls, his life would be complete. We got to the Via Veneto with all of its sophisticated restaurants and boutiques as well as some high-end residences. This was one of the few places where we saw expensive private homes in the city. I suspect many of the wealthier folks live away from tourist sections.

At the end of the Via Veneto we were right across the street from one of the long sidewalks of the Villa Borghese. From the street it looked like a massive, rectangular property with long bucolic walkways studded with benches and some vendors with carts. When we got to the far end we found the museum and a path that passed other buildings, some of which seemed to have screened-in flight cages for birds on the roofs. At the opposite end of the path from the museum was a zoo. We decided to have a little lunch on the grounds and then go for a walk through the zoo.

While we were having lunch, Dino asked, "Who was that guy that had the big hit record and then you never heard from him again?" I told him I didn't know, I hadn't heard from the guy since he had that big hit record. I also pointed out that his description could apply to about 140 singers in the last fifty years, so maybe he could narrow it down a little. He added that the album came out in the '70s, or maybe the '80s, and it wasn't a band, but it might have been. So now the race was on, the gauntlet had been thrown. Who could think of the guy, or band, first. Cathy disqualified herself, saying she wasn't sure if she knew, but she was positive she didn't care. It was down to Dino, Carolyn, and me. I was sure I could do it; I just had to stop thinking about it. And then, twenty minutes later, out of nowhere, while we were walking along, Carolyn went up to Dino, smacked him on the back, and blurted out, "Boz Scaggs, *Silk Degrees*, 'Lido Shuffle.'" Dino said, "That's it, you got it, and you beat Pete … never hit me again. I almost felt that."

My stomach was still feeling a little queasy, so while the other three ate sandwiches, I had a bottle of water. I noticed some unfamiliar birds feeding nearby. Dino could see I was observing the birds closely and asked, "Petey, you know what they call those birds?" In a momentary lapse of judgment I walked right into the set up and said, "No, what?" Dino replied, "Fucking sparrows."

With that we went to the zoo. It was relatively small, but Dino noticed signs that indicated there were wolves, or *lupi*, in one part of the zoo. For some reason, that was all Dino wanted to see, the lupi. So of course, that was the one thing we couldn't find. There were giant rats, giraffes, and some other funky residents, but try as we might, we could not find those stupid lupi. After the third loop through the zoo, Carolyn had had enough.

Carolyn: "That's it, if the lupi aren't around this next turn, we're walking back to the museum."

Dino: "But you said we could see the lupi, Carolyn."

Carolyn: "I'm sorry, Dino, but I'm tired of looking for the damn things, and I want to see the museum. I don't even like lupies."

We turned the corner and found ourselves at the same dead

end by the monkeys we'd hit three other times. Off in the distance, a couple of lupi laughed … or cried.

Carolyn: "That's it, let's go."

Dino: "But we didn't see the lupi. They've got to be nearby. I can hear them."

Carolyn: "Dino, I think they're piping in lupi noise just to piss you off."

Dino: "It's working."

Carolyn: "Let's go. Maybe if we get through the museum quickly enough we can come back and see the lupi later."

Dino: "Aaah, you won't come back. This is a f*@#ing rip off."

Carolyn: "Dino, we've had a really nice time, don't ruin it."

Dino: "Carolyn, Carolyn, Carolyn, what happened to you? You used to do whatever I told you."

Carolyn: "Fuck the lupi, Dino, let's go."

We sauntered off to the museum. I think maybe the prospect of seeing nude paintings and sculpture got Dino's mind off the lupi for a few minutes. Unfortunately, the museum was crowded, and we had to go downstairs to check our bags and jackets and get tickets before we could get in. By this time the walking and the vain search for lupi had taken a toll on Cathy's back. The museum had elevators, but of course today they weren't working. So while we zipped around looking at Caravaggios and other great pieces of art, Cathy was stuck trying to find a place to sit. The most striking piece of sculpture I saw was Canova's sculpture of Pauline Bonaparte reclining on a settee. The cushion of the settee was so realistic you would swear it was a mattress instead of white marble. I called Dino over to look at it. He stared at the piece and said, "Nice rack." At least he wasn't complaining about the lupi.

The museum was open and airy, which made it a very pleasant visit. By the time we were done, Cathy's back was feeling a little better. We walked behind the museum to see the formal gardens, but they were being cut back in preparation for fall flowers. While I'm sure the gardens look great when they are in bloom, a bunch of dried stubs didn't really hold our interest, so we headed back toward the hotel by what looked like a more direct path along Via Quattro Fontagne. Early in the walk, as it appeared we were on the right track, Dino said, "Petey, normally I wouldn't make a big deal about this, and I am a little uncomfortable saying it, but you've done a good job getting us around." I was smart enough not to get a big head, and about five minutes later, Rome turned into freaking San Francisco. I had read about the Seven Hills of Rome. All of them seemed to be between our hotel and the Villa Borghese. Couldn't they number them and have warning signs, "You are approaching hill number 4, get a cab"? As the streets got steeper, I kept thinking Cathy would be in agony, but if she was, she hid it pretty well.

When we got back to our neighborhood, we decided to inquire about train tickets for Florence, which was the next stop on our trip and also where our younger daughter, Jackie was studying art for the semester. So Carolyn and I waited outside while Mr. Rosetta Stone and his wife went into a little visitors and transportation office. When they came out, Dino reported that a rail strike was scheduled for the next day, Saturday, but that it would last only that day and we should be OK for our Sunday train. That struck me as a little odd. I could understand scheduling a strike, but scheduling when it would end seemed to defeat its purpose. But who was I to argue with a system that hadn't worked for three hundred years?

All of us were tired when we got back to the hotel. Dino had heard from the front desk manager that Santa Christina was a very good restaurant about a half mile away, so we decided to give it a try after a nap and a shower. Dino and I met in the lobby for wine. Cathy came down a short time later. Dino, irritated, asked me, "Where's Carolyn?" I looked around the room and said, "Not here." I couldn't go back up to the room, because Carolyn had the keys and I didn't have any more jewelry with me. So we just cooled our heels until "Where's Carolyn" came downstairs. The best part was, the more it aggravated Dino, the more Carolyn seemed to enjoy it.

We walked over to Santa Christina, which was a little hard to find because it was hidden; tucked away among some larger buildings. All the way over it looked like the sky was about to open up and pour on us, but we got to the restaurant before it started sprinkling. After we were seated, the rain came down in buckets, but the restaurant was great. The chicken gorgonzola and beef Wellington each got four stars. How do they get that much flavor without drowning the stuff in sauce? The rain let up only a little, so we ran most of the way back to the hotel. That is an exaggeration of the highest order, but we did get back quickly for us. We had wine and talked in the D'Adamos' room until 1 a.m. We avoided politics and instead Dino explained why being nice wasn't worth the effort. He told us that by the end of the trip the three if us would see things his way and be miserable bastards just like him. I couldn't wait.

Back in our room, I started working from the notes I had made, building on this idea that I could move to Rome. The city is laid out with scores of ancient wonders nestled among modern conveniences and tourist accommodations. It is easy to forget that there are probably many more artifacts still buried or unwittingly destroyed by prior generations. I started thinking that maybe the same happens with people. Generation after generation adding layers of history and folklore so that the current generations bear little resemblance to their ancestors. Maybe my ancestors weren't all from this country, but maybe being here I could get to know the real me. If I was at all inebriated before that thought crossed my mind, I was completely sober after. Why the hell would I want to tamper with the carefully crafted façade that had served me so well all these years? I guarantee you there would be no laughs in that exercise. No, moving to Italy and getting to know myself was scary enough to me, let alone writing it down to share with anybody else. I went further through my notes of the day, like when Dino complained about not finding the Lupi. I think the idea of moving to Italy appealed to me because Dino was going to eventually leave here and maybe never come back. Tomorrow we would go to the Vatican. Maybe God would give me a hint.

September 12: According to Dino

Today, we decide to hit the Villa Borghese. It's not too far, so we walk, and once again I find it awesome that we're actually strolling through Rome, Italy. I never get used to it. Everywhere we look there's something different than what we would be able to see at home. We pass one building where a flock of nuns are milling about (I'm not sure what the right term is for a bunch of nuns? A gaggle? A herd?). Suddenly a bell rings, and they all disappear through the front door. When I say disappear I don't mean that they walked inside. I mean they really disappeared. Doors were still closed and they floated right through them. Then again, I hadn't eaten anything yet so maybe it was my imagination.

As we walk, I notice that almost all of the buildings look ancient, and probably are, but housed within them are upscale clothing stores and modern offices. This marriage of ancient and modern blows me away. Then, every block or so, there's a small shrine carved into a wall with fresh-cut flowers that someone stuck into them. Below them you usually see a very old stone fountain. They all still work, and the water tastes clear and fresh.

Crucifixes are carved into the walls, frescoes of saints are everywhere, and every religious symbol imaginable can be seen within a few yards of each other. It dawns on me that the Italian Chapter of the ACLU must be asleep at the wheel. Isn't it remarkable that in America we remove all religious evidence from everything because we're afraid that someone who doesn't believe in God might be offended, but Italy has millions of people visiting every year just to see it all?

Like every other walk in Rome, this one is an adventure as we simply take in all of the unique and different sites that surround us as we walk. Half the population of Rome rides scooters—Vespas, Piaggios, Hondas, and a dozen other brands. The cars are supposed to obey the traffic signs and signals (Italian drivers say these are merely suggestions), but the scooters don't have to. I see that many of the scooters have little decals of people's faces on their sides.

Some have a "T" under them, some don't. I learn that the "T" stands for "tourist." It's like the decals that they used to put on the side of World War II fighter jets when they shot down an enemy plane. Here's the wild thing: I can understand them trying to hit a tourist. That's only fair. But they put decals on when they hit another Italian! That's sick! That would be like an Italian pilot in the war landing his plane and the guy on the ground says

Ground guy: "Hey Gino, how'd you do?"

Gino: "Good, I shoota down fivea planes. Two enemy, and three of our own."

Ground guy, as he pats Gino on the back: "Bene, bene !"

The best are the Italian women who hike up their already short skirts, straddle those babies, and, with their four-inch high heels, navigate through anything in their way. Just the sight of one of them would cause a twenty-car pileup back home, but here it's part of life. La dolce vita.

I immediately curse my ancestors for coming to America. What were they thinking? I then start thinking that I might pay a visit to my grandfather's small home town, Castel Forte, outside of Rome one day. After looking at a map, however, I find that his description of the town as just outside of Rome is a little off. To me it looks a lot closer to Naples. If I were him, I'd lie too. I'm thinking that visiting the town would still be a good idea, when suddenly I have a vision of a wrinkled old Italian sitting on a wooden box with goats standing all around him looking at me and saying;

Old Italian guy: "Olivio D'Adamo was your grandfather?"

Dino: "Yes, he was."

Old Italian guy: "He owes me money!"

Suddenly, this doesn't sound like such a good idea anymore. So I continue following the Grecos, against my better judgment, until finally we arrive at the park that leads to the Villa Borghese. Panini and Italian sodas are available from trucks located along the park trails. We grab some of this truck lunch (which, I have to admit, is not as good as the Taylor pork roll and fried-egg truck sandwiches that I'm used to) and decide we'll hit the Borghese Zoo before we do the museum. So we stroll through the entrance, and the first thing we see is the monkey cage. I don't know what I was expecting—it's not like I thought the monkeys would chatter with an Italian accent or anything (but I'll be damned if they didn't use their little hands more than American monkeys do)—but the zoo is pretty much what you'd see anywhere. In one pen we see huge rodents that are the biggest things this side of Newark, New Jersey. That's something. But all I want to see are the wolves. I don't know why, but I don't think I ever saw wolves in a zoo before. One simple request: I wanna see the lupi. I was promised by everyone that if I just kept quiet, I'd see the lupi. Never happened. I'm pissed—still am.

So sans lupi, I enter the Villa Borghese, a great museum with fantastic sculptures. The busts of the Roman emperors are made out of different types and colors of marble, each type used separately to depict their faces, their robes, etc. Admiring these beautiful statues make me wonder why I never see anything this artistic that's been done within the last two hundred years. Now we have thirteen-foot clothespins, or 109 orange sheets hanging in Central Park, and we call that art.

The Villa Borghese houses a magnificent collection of artwork, but it's already a few hours since we've eaten, and I'm thinking about dinner. A half hour later we start to make our way out of the museum, which is good because if I hear Carolyn say "awesome" one more time, I'm going to kill myself, or more likely her. So I go over to Pete and pinch his ass. I'm pretty sly about it, and every time I do this, I make sure he thinks it's Cathy. Poor guy, let him dream.

On the way back to the hotel, we stop at a little one-room structure on the street that looks like a place to buy train tickets.

The person behind the desk doesn't speak English, so I give my Italian a try. I discover that although I can almost make myself understood, I can't understand the answers, which kind of defeats the purpose. Luckily, a lady comes in and tells us in English that a strike is scheduled for tomorrow, but it will be over by the next day. Very civilized, don't you think? It's like a way to schedule a vacation day whenever you want one. I make a mental note to give this a shot as soon as I get back home.

We return to the hotel and ask the desk guy (translation: concierge/valet who is neither but is very good at watching TV), who tries to ignore us, where we can get a good dinner *in vicino* (in the area). I almost tell him I want a good spot for Italian food but catch myself just in time. I never would have heard the end of that one. (The Grecos and my beautiful wife have so few things to crack on me about that they tend to totally overdo those few things when I truly do screw something up). So ten minutes later, when his favorite television show breaks for a commercial, he recommends Santa Christina as the best restaurant in the area. I think that's bullshit because he probably gets paid to recommend it, but then again I think everybody's on the take. On the other hand, how bad could a restaurant be if it's named after a saint? We head over, and it's a cozy place in a little square behind some commercial buildings. It's a little scary getting to it through a dark alley, so we let the girls go first. The place turns out to be wonderful, just like every other eating establishment in this wonderful freaking country. I can't remember what I ate, but I suspect Pete wrote it down somewhere. Anyway, it's great, and as always the vino is flowing like *acqua*, the Grecos are engaged in pleasant conversation with my wife, and everybody leaves me alone. I'm in heaven. A phrase my grandfather used to say comes to mind. *Una tavola senza vino e come una giornata senza sole* (a table without wine is like a day without sunshine). How true, grand pop, how true.

That night we all end up in our room and polish off the grappa. OK, technically it's only me drinking the grappa. Pete and the girls enjoy a nice dessert wine we pick up in a little trattoria on the way back.

I'm really rubbing it into the Grecos that we have a balcony and they don't, when my wife tells me that we had to pay extra for the damn thing. So now, the Grecos are at our room every night because we have the balcony, drinking my booze AND impeding on my Italian porn time, which is my favorite channel on the little Italian TV—and the only one I can understand without subtitles.

Saturday, September 13: Peter's Version

The weather was absolutely sparkling as we boarded a bus on Via Nazionale for the Vatican. Carolyn had spent weeks—wait, no, twenty minutes—researching and arranging a guided tour of the Vatican for us. It didn't start until 1 p.m., so we stopped and had tea and croissants at an outdoor café. The weather couldn't have been nicer, and we strolled around the front of the Vatican for a while. This was one image that was pretty much as we all had pictured it. As the time for the tour approached, we had a little trouble figuring out where it was we should meet the tour guide. According to our information, we had to go behind the Vatican. It felt a little like we were behind the curtain at a theme park; go two hundred yards to the right of the Vatican and there's no sidewalk, just a couple of storefronts, and a lot of Italians looking at us like we just broke security at a rock concert. Carolyn and I were walking ahead of Dino and Cathy. There was nothing nice to see on this side street. Carolyn is usually a little under-confident, and now she was beginning to think she was in the wrong place. She wasn't afraid of missing the tour; she was afraid of Dino's reaction.

"What is he going to do when we have to turn around and go back because I led us the wrong way?" she asked.

"Just tell them it was my fault, and you are fixing it," I replied.

"We do that a lot with him; don't you think he'll suspect something?" Carolyn asked.

"Are you kidding? Dino blames everything on me. At dinner last night he blamed me for the humidity, remember?"

But just then, across the street from an entrance to the Vatican Museum, we saw the outdoor stairway that was on the directions. Carolyn turned back to Dino and Cathy and casually said, "Yep, here it is, just like I thought."

Yeah.

Carolyn and I walked down the steps to make sure it was the right place. The tour company had instructed us to look for a girl with a blue folder. It would have been easier if they had told us to look for the girl with pink hair, one green shoe, one orange shoe, eleven tattoos, and a pierced nose holding a blue folder, but that's just me.

We found the girl (who was from California) and told her that Dino and Cathy were with us but waiting for us at the top of the stairs. I wanted to tell her they weren't real bright and hadn't really figured out how stairs work, but I'm such a wimp I knew I wouldn't be able to get that out without laughing. So I told her they were really arrogant and didn't want to be seen with all the common tourists. I did add that they weren't really smart, so the guide would have to speak very slowly. She smiled and clearly had me pegged as the jackass of her group.

Fortunately she wasn't the tour guide, she just got us to the tour guide. His name was John. He was in his late twenties, had moved to Rome from New York about seven years earlier to go to school, and had decided to stay.

Now, as I mentioned, this was the only part of the vacation that Carolyn was in charge of, and she was really hoping it would go well. The twenty or so people in our group walked into the Vatican Museum, and John started the tour. He began his spiel, and Cathy, Dino, and Carolyn really seemed to enjoy it. The guy was very entertaining and a little irreverent, and, I began to suspect, a little full of shit. He was mentioning which pope had begun building the Sistine Chapel and that one of Michelangelo's rivals had arranged for him to get the job illustrating its ceiling because Michelangelo was a sculptor, not a painter. That way Michelangelo would fail and be humiliated, and the rival would get the job. While we stopped for Dino to take pictures of a trash can, I quietly asked John, "If this rival had enough influence to get Michelangelo the job, why didn't he just get it for himself and save the time?" John answered, "Ahh, yes, but the pope's sister Patty knew of this and … OK everybody, let's head over to the sculpture with all the snakes!"

One of the impressive sights was the Belvedere Torso. Or as John called it, "The great sculpture that we don't know anything about, which got broken." This is judged to be one of the greatest feats of sculpting. Dino got some great pictures from a variety of angles, moving around like a fashion photographer and telling other tourists to get the fuck out of his shot, which they did.

John mixed in enough facts, like "the Vatican is a very popular tourist attraction" and, "You'll notice much of the writing is in Italian or Latin," that you felt like you were learning stuff. But when he said he was forbidden from actually entering the Sistine Chapel, *the essential reason for the freaking tour,* because of a contractual agreement between his tour company and the Italian government, I knew he was a phony. I mean, come on—*what* Italian government? Finally, we saw the Raphael fresco in the room leading to the chapel itself. This was a magnificent piece of art with depictions of Michelangelo, Galileo, Socrates, and Raphael himself. John tried to tell me that one of the figures was Abraham Lincoln, but by this point I had given up challenging him.

Eventually we came to the Sistine Chapel. John spotted a guard, ducked into the crowd, and ran away. Earlier in the tour John had told us that photography was forbidden in the Sistine Chapel. Of course when we walked in we couldn't hear ourselves think above the clicking and whirring of cameras. In order to preserve the artwork, no artificial light is allowed in the room. Dino's camera did a much better job than ours of catching the colors in the natural light. My pictures looked like a Moody Blues album cover.

While walking through the chapel, I played out how Dino would complain about John's tour guiding so I would be ready for any of the eventual insults. Knowing Dino, there were three or four obvious categories of comments, and before too long I was all set with a comeback for each category. This left plenty of time to appreciate the famous ceiling. Even in the dull, late afternoon light, you could notice the detail and perspective of this massive undertaking. Michelangelo developed his own scaffolding technique to enable him to paint his way and he abandoned the customary templates, painting directly on the ceiling without guides. I learned that when I got home. The minute we stepped outside, Dino said, "I don't know how that fucking tour guide did it, but I know less about the Vatican now than I did when I got here." I was all set: "That's impossible, Dino." Evidently the comeback was better than he anticipated, and he only brought it up ten or fifteen more times the rest of the trip.

Once outside the chapel, we were free to go to Saint Peter's Basilica, but first we bought some holy memorabilia, just like the Apostles did when they toured Rome to promote their first album in 38 AD. I almost bought a Pope Benedict XVI baseball cap and a "Go

Catholics" foam finger, but I went with a handful of little crucifixes instead. We went into the basilica, and it seemed less organized than I thought it would be. Pews and altars were scattered everywhere, and you couldn't swing a dead cat without hitting a sepulcher for an old pope. It was very impressive, but I had imagined there would be miles of aisles facing the front. In fact, they were setting up for a 5:30 mass, and fewer than two hundred folding chairs were aimed at the altar that was going to be used. We thought about staying for mass, but every mass I ever saw televised from the Vatican was a two or three hour long Gregorian chant top-forty deal. Plus, I thought it would be nice to go to some little local church near the hotel, forgetting that I would be relying on Mario to know where to find a mass on a Sunday in the capital of the Catholic Church. So we took pictures 147 through 196 in the area in front of the basilica and headed for the bus to the hotel.

When we got back to the hotel I turned on my Blackberry for the first time since we got to Rome. I had sent my kids a text message when we landed and decided to turn the thing off for a few days. Now when I checked my e-mail I saw a message from my friend Danny whose literary agent friend Paul would be meeting me in Venice in ten days. Evidently, Danny had shared some of my newspaper pieces with Paul and he was very enthusiastic about the possibilities for the Italy book. Paul told Danny to tell me he was especially interested to see what fresh, creative approach I would take on a fairly common subject like travel to Italy. "Fresh and creative approach?" I thought I just had to be funny. For fresh and creative I would need about six more weeks and a lot more talent. I like writing when I have a little pressure, but I also like writing when I have a clue. I was going to have to start giving this more attention because with ten days to go I had nothing.

That night, as we started out looking for a local restaurant, a block from our hotel we saw a good-looking girl standing in a doorway, waving something at us, and gesturing for us to come inside. At first I thought she was a prostitute waving a list of specials, but I don't really know exactly what a prostitute looks like. I asked Dino. I can't repeat what he said because my Mom might read this book someday.

Anyway, the girl wasn't a prostitute. She was waving restaurant menus, not excerpts from the *Kama Sutra*. The place, called al Boschetta, looked nice, so we went for it. In the front room there was a big salad-bar-type display of olives, artichokes, and similar nutritious—and therefore personally unappealing—items. We were led to a room that seemed to be a courtyard with a canopy over it. When I looked up at the canopy, I saw a cat walking along the supports. Now, Dino and Cathy have approximately forty pets, so I didn't think they would mind a cat in the restaurant. But I was a little concerned about Carolyn, so I didn't say anything—until the cat sat down on a beam right above our heads and I blurted out, "Holy shit, look at that cat!" As a testament to how relaxed she was at this point, Carolyn didn't mind. The cat seemed to be an employee of the restaurant rather than an escaped entrée. It just looked down at the diners and took note of what items were and weren't moving that night. It was our first of three cat encounters of the trip.

The menus in Rome were much broader than I expected. At al Boschetta the menu included lamb and osso buco (slowly cooked veal shanks in a savory sauce served over risotto), and for the first time I tried bucatini all'Amatriciana; thick spaghetti in a sauce of pecorino cheese, paprika, and pancetta. Dino and I wondered why more American restaurants weren't featuring this wonderful dish. It isn't expensive to make and has such a distinctive flavor.

While we were eating, I mentioned that the vacation was really working out great so far. Dino told me to speak for myself, but I was feeling pretty brave and continued. We started discussing why things were going so well. At the end we all agreed that it comes down to two things. First, you can't try to cram ten pounds of marbles into a five-pound bag. You pick out the few things you really need to see and do, leave some time for doing nothing here and there, and if there is a nice surprise, great. Second, we all came here with the idea of just experiencing Italy, not inspecting it. There is a lot to enjoy just by becoming part of somebody else's world and leaving yours behind. That was what we had done so far, and what we would do the rest of the trip. At that point, Dino told me to shut up and pass the wine. After dinner, I went with the subtle yet determined panna cotta gelato as the perfect complement to our philosophical discussion and the all'Amatriciana.

When we got back to the hotel, I asked Mario if there was a Catholic church nearby. He seemed confused by the idea of going to church on Sunday in Rome and said he would check and get back to me in the morning. That would be the last time we saw Mario. Rumor has it he got lost going home—which was next door—and ended up modeling for priest calendars in Calabria.

September 13: According to Dino

As already stated, my wife, Cathy, had worked out all the details for the entire trip. She's Oriental, and they are known to have a strong attention to detail. We all know this is true, because Chinese menus are so well organized that they actually have little columns, and all the meals are numbered.

Funny story about Chinese menus: We're at a Chinese restaurant in Hawaii once, and one of my sons tells me to look at meal number thirty-seven in column three. I crack up because it says "Fookin chicken." That was it. For the rest of the trip, everything we ate was preceded by "fookin": "I feel like a fookin hamburger, how 'bout you?" Or, "Who's up for some fookin eggs?" We never got tired of it.

So where was I? Ah yes, I was saying that my wife is detail-oriented because she's Oriental. She actually get's angry when I call her Oriental. She says the only Oriental thing in our house is the rug. She says people are *Asian*. Jeez. Those Orientals are so fookin sensitive. Anyway, Carolyn has this one thing to do on the whole trip, which is to organize the Vatican tour. I figure, what the hell, I'm not Catholic, so it doesn't matter if she screws it up, which I'm certain she will.

Funny story about me not being Catholic: When my grandmother's mother and father came to America from Italy, the score was: daughters 5, money 0. The Protestant Church took care of them, so my great-grandfather announced (to no one in particular; he did that a lot) that from that day forward they would all be Protestant (but with an Italian accent: "Froma disa day fowarde ..."—you get the picture). And that was what came to pass. When my grandfather married my grandmother, he was Catholic, but he stayed in the closet. It wasn't until his funeral, when a priest gave the eulogy (which should have been our first clue), that we all found out he would go to Mass during the week, and gave money to the Catholic Church. Who knew? Boy, were we fookin pissed! So aside from my grandfather, the closet Catholic,

I think my family are the only Italian Protestants in the world. It was tough being the only Italians in a Protestant church. It was like being the only black people in Selma, Alabama. We had a separate collection plate that said, "Italians Only," and had to sit in the last pew.

So getting back to Carolyn, she books the tour, and Cathy and I are following Pete and her as they try to figure out where the hell we're supposed to meet the tour. I can tell from how they're walking that they have no clue where they're going, but they're trying to cover it up by turning around and smiling and nodding their heads at us every two minutes. They looked like two escapees from the fookin loony bin. Finally they quicken their pace, like two rat terriers that have just picked up a scent, and we can see that they have actually found our tour guide, who, by the way, looks like another escapee from the same loony bin. The girl is a walking rainbow. You'd think at least one of the several colors she's wearing would match her hair (bright pink by the way), but that, alas, was not in the cards. Thank God, we don't have to get too close, as Cathy's back is hurting and she doesn't want to go down the steps to where the rest of the tour huddles together like a herd of nuns. The Grecos went down to meet her, and pretty soon the whole group of about twenty-five people is waving to us. I can tell that Pete is probably making fun of me, but I know that we are between them and the Vatican, so unless the tour is being done through binoculars they'll all eventually have to trudge back up the steps.

Pretty soon the girl with pink hair blows a whistle, and they come up the steps to where Cathy and I are sitting and eating lemon gelatos. Suckers! Pete and Carolyn introduce us to the actual tour guide, who's an American. The psychedelic chick is just his assistant (her qualification, evidently, is that on weekends she plays lead whistle in an Italian reggae band). Now why Carolyn picks an American tour guide for the Vatican deal is beyond me, unless we get some "I don't know shit" discount, which we don't.

Fortunately, we don't need the guide that much anyway. The

Vatican is really awesome. The vast open area in front of it is named Piazza San Pietro. It's in the shape of a gigantic ellipse, surrounded by columns with statues of saints on top, more than a hundred of them.

In the middle of the plaza stands a towering Egyptian obelisk that was either moved from Nero's Circus or taken from Egypt by Marc Antony, depending on which tour guide you believe. Ours said it was a movie prop leftover from *The Da Vinci Code*. Go up the steps and you're in Saint Peter's Basilica, the largest church in the world and unbelievably majestic. I'm snapping pictures like a Japanese school girl when I see a little old Italian nun kneeling in front of a small altar off to the side. A very private and moving scene. So poignant and I quietly snap a picture. I think I'll have the photo enlarged when I get home and done in four frames like an Andy Warhol thing. Maybe hang it over the couch.

Suffice it to say that even though the church seems more of a tourist attraction than a holy shrine, I think that, depending on your attitude, you can either just be blown away by the art and design or be overwhelmed by the spiritual significance. You don't have to be Catholic to feel the presence of God there… I know. I know he's everywhere. I just don't sense him quite as strongly when I'm getting my tires rotated or mowing the lawn.

Cathy's thirsty, so I buy her a bottle of Holy Water. Tasted the same as regular water to me, but Cathy swore that one of my horns got shorter. Orientals can be funny when they want to.

The Vatican Museum and the Sistine Chapel are unbelievable: I can't imagine anywhere on Earth that has more examples of the best artwork ever done. Huge and beautiful frescoes adorn the walls. I can't stop staring at *The School of Athens*, by Raphael. The architecture is jaw-dropping, and even some of the floors are covered by mosaics that portray exquisitely detailed images. The incredible paintings and sculptures that were done hundreds of years ago are everywhere you look, and it is still a mystery to me why we seem to have lost that ability in modern times. Of all the sculptures we see, and there were many, many beautiful ones, my favorite is the Torso. Supposedly, it is thousands of years old and was unearthed during Michelangelo's time. According to the story, when Michelangelo saw it he almost stopped sculpting because he claimed he could never do anything better. This, from The Man— the guy who sculpted *David*, the famous statue that we will see in Florence and the most awe-inspiring thing I have ever experienced. And the Torso is by someone we never even heard of, thousands of years ago. Crazy (Pazzo). Of course, the highlight of the Vatican is the ceiling of the Sistine Chapel, which has scores of panels, each illustrating a different biblical theme. The center panel, the one we call "The Creation", is the most famous, but the depictions that cover the entire ceiling are awesome as well. Took the master four years to complete the entire ceiling, and unbelievably, he considered himself a sculptor rather than a painter. What I also found staggering was that Michelangelo actually invented the scaffolding system that enabled him to accomplish the work. The scaffolding that he created is actually the basis of what we still use today. I tell my wife this but she insists that the Asians invented scaffolding. She said the same thing about ice cream, fireworks, and even pasta. Asians are very insecure, in case you don't know, and lie about almost everything.

The Vatican, of course, is a separate country, and the Pope is guarded by Swiss Guards. Now call me crazy, but if you're not going to use local Italian talent, wouldn't you want German guards, or maybe Russian guards? In wars, aren't the Swiss always "neutral"? Ooooh, the Swiss. Don't want to mess with the Swiss. Come on, they're the last nationality I'd pick to have my back. Well, maybe not the last. The French would be last. But definitely the next to last.

At the end of the tour, we all go to the Vatican gift shop. I buy some T-shirts that say "Catholics Do it Better" and "My Parents Saw the Pope and All He Blessed Was This Crummy Tee Shirt" and a couple of postcards. Called it a day.

Trudged back to the hotel. Took a nice nap. Got up. Went downstairs where I see Mario. He pours me a glass of wine before

I even sit down. The pistachios are there before I can ask for them. I keep repeating, "I love my wife, I love my wife." Then Mario puts the bottle of Chianti in front of me and says, "Hey Dino, there's a little left. You finish, eh?"

I start to say, "I love my ..." but then realize, what the hell, our marriage isn't perfect. We even went to counseling once. It didn't work, we're still married. Here's how it went. We're sitting on two ends of a couch in the counselor's office and the counselor says, "OK, let's talk about what you feel is lacking in the marriage." She starts with Cathy. Big mistake. Three weeks later we sit down again, and Cathy continues with number 111 on her list. She starts number 112, but hesitates and then says, "Actually this one isn't really that important. I guess I'm done." This takes me by surprise, as I wasn't thinking I'd ever get up to bat. Even the counselor seems a little unprepared for the sudden ending of Cathy's litany of issues, which were starting to sound like a sequel to *Dante's Inferno*. Anyway, the counselor tries to regain her composure and says, "Well, thank you, Cathy." She then looks at me.

> Counselor: "Dino, what would you like to see in the marriage?"
>
> Dino: "I'd like to come home from work one day and have her answer the door in a French maid's outfit."
>
> Counselor: "So, you're looking for more spontaneous, more creative sex?"
>
> Dino: "No. I'd just like her to clean the house."

Anyway, now I'm trying to justify why I should leave my wonderful wife and start playing for the other team, when it occurs to me that Mario is probably not gay anyway. Dean Martin comes on my iPhone singing "Que Sera, Sera." I slowly turn up the volume. "Sing it, Dino. Sing it." The Grecos and Cathy come down, and I give her my best "I wasn't sitting here thinking of leaving you" look. She buys it, and we're off to dinner. All thoughts of Mario are lost with the antipasto. We picked a restaurant we passed the night before and are led to the back of the place to an area that doesn't have a roof. In other words, it's behind the restaurant. Pete points to a cat walking along a ledge, and he thinks it's cool that they let a cat in the restaurant. I don't tell him that we're not in a restaurant. It's the back yard of a restaurant, and there are probably raccoons here, too. That wouldn't be so cute, would it, Pete? Big-ass rodent jumping on your lap, dragging off your osso buco?

The *il primo* course is pasta with sauce all'Amatriciana. It's incredible. I can't believe I've never had this before, and in fact have never even heard of it. I'm thinking about opening up a Pasta All'Amatriciana franchise back home. Maybe Mario could run it. He sneaks back into my thoughts, that little scamp.

When the waiter asks what I want for *il secondo*, I say, "Let it ride, Giuseppe." Everyone else gets veal and steak, but I don't care. I order another plate of the same. The house wine is splendid. The little naps we all took has us feeling pretty perky, despite the marathon day at the Vatican, and our normal three-hour dinner stretches to four. Everyone shares spoonfuls of everyone else's desserts, and we finally drain the last of our decaf espressos. We are the last ones at the restaurant, so we think it prudent to call it a night and drag ourselves back to our rooms. Buona notte, Roma.

Sunday, September 14: Peter's Version

In spite of Mario's help, Carolyn and I found a church and went inside to pray for a little while. After expiating our shared, inbred Catholic guilt and me praying for inspiration for this godforsaken book, we ate breakfast at a café at Piazza del Monti. Dino and Cathy had decided to go to an outdoor market across the Tiber and we agreed to meet at lunch time. We figured out how to get to Santa Maria Cosmedin, the little church which is also the site of the famous Boca Della Veritas, or Mouth of Truth. We got to the neighborhood of the Mouth of Truth, but decided to wait until Dino and Cathy could join us before going inside. The Mouth of Truth is famous in Rome and received some international exposure in the film *Roman Holiday* starring Gregory Peck and Audrey Hepburn. Built into the wall outside of the church is a bas relief of the face of Truth. Legend has it that if you answer a question falsely and put your hand in the mouth, it will devour your hand

While we waited to meet up with the D'Adamos, we explored the area along the Tiber south of the Vatican. We found three more streets with the name "Greco" in them, and a couple of restaurants too. We decided not to tell Dino unless he got annoying. We walked along the Tiber River and went back and forth across a couple of bridges. There was a small waterfall beneath one of the footbridges and bobbing around at the base of the waterfall were a dozen plastic soft drink bottles of different colors. There were greens, reds, blues, and even more exotic hues. Sizes and shapes varied too. They all danced and bobbed in the gently tumbling water. Even the trash looked good here.

We got a text from Cathy telling us to meet them on one of the bridges so we can have lunch in a nearby piazza. It was easy to get around Rome—now that we were getting ready to leave it. We found them easily enough and there was an open square area where we found a little bistro for lunch. There Cathy gave Carolyn a little lidded bowl for sugar packets. Carolyn had mentioned wanting to get one on the first day, and Cathy remembered. Picking up little things that people say and then acting on them is one of Cathy's endearing traits. Dino didn't mind the nice gesture, but wished Cathy hadn't taken the price tag off the bottom of the bowl before she gave it to Carolyn. We shared a delicious lunch of salad and calamari, then had a casual walk back over to Santa Maria Cosmedin so we could all experience the Mouth of Truth.

The line doubled back around an iron gate that paralleled the front of the building. Inside the gate, an older man sat at a table making ocarina's from clay, playing them as a way to drum up interest. He was selling them for five Euros. I decided to buy one, and as I was getting the money out of my pocket, I saw an eight- or nine-year-old boy looking at the old man. He was clearly fascinated by the work and the ocarinas. So, summoning up all the Italian that Dino had taught me, I said, "Due," gave the man ten Euros, and pointed to the boy. The man gave him one ocarina and me the other. The boy was happy and said, "Grazie," I felt good. Then the boy tried playing the damn ocarina the entire time we stood in line and the rest of the people in the queue turned into a United Nations of cursing all aimed at me. Dino put his arm on my shoulder and said something to the crowd in Italian, and everybody applauded. Evidently he told them it was wrong of me to buy the ocarina, but on the other hand I hadn't peed my pants all day, and he was very proud of me. The crowd smiled at me and I thanked him.

The Mouth of Truth looked just like we had pictured it, and we took the requisite photographs: innocently putting a hand near it, screaming with a hand inside (Carolyn's, not mine— I refused to put my hand in there. I don't put my extremities in too many places. This thing could have been called the Mouth of Money, and I wouldn't have tried it.).

Anyway, after that we went inside to look at the little church. There were items on display that didn't seem to have any special significance, nor were they especially interesting to look at or attractively displayed. Maybe they were in the process of getting set up for some big event? This would be the only time on our trip when it seemed someone had just thrown together random crap to justify the cost of a ticket. But it was Sunday, so I kept that thought to myself.

Behind the Mouth of Truth and Rip-off Chapel, we arrived at the Circus Maximus. I didn't come to the Circus Maximus with an image in my mind, but I half expected a ruined building and maybe the remains of a chariot out of which thirty or forty clowns would have emerged during the height of the show. But such was not the case. This was more the Great Big Yard of Maximus. It was a long wide field, maybe five or six acres in all, with a lot of the grass worn away by people walking through with their dogs. There were people jogging and generally hanging out. We stared at the site for a few seconds thinking that maybe something would happen; nope. Caesar would be pissed.

Back in front of Santa Maria Cosmedin we were able to catch the 170 bus to the Stazione Termini to get our tickets for the train to Florence. We took the 170 because I had stayed up late cramming for the final exam in Intro to Bus Logistics and knew exactly where it went and where to get it. I couldn't afford another colossal mistake. It was a good idea to get the tickets the day before we were leaving because it gave us a feel for the station. It was laid out the way you might imagine a train station from movies in the '40s and '50s would be with high ceilings, a café with seating on the marble floor and ticket counters with metal bars instead of sound proofed Plexiglas barriers. The only problem was that a couple of us had to use the bathroom. The signs indicated the restrooms were downstairs. We followed sign after sign after sign, which eventually led us, I think, to Belgium. When we got to the restrooms we discovered they required exact change (about sixty cents). I try not to perform any delicate function while I'm angry. It makes me clumsy. But I peed angry that day and it felt right…

We found our way back to the front entrance, and got on the right bus returning to the hotel at about 4 p.m. and did some preliminary packing. Then we all met in the lobby about 5:30 and decided to go back to the Trevi Fountain. It was beautiful in the late afternoon light. As we left the area, Cathy decided to look for a store she had seen on our first day in Rome, to get a gift for one of her boys. With Cathy and Carolyn leading the way—for the next twenty minutes—we took a series of turns, each of which ended with us returning to the Trevi Fountain. Except for the time we wound up at a dead end. This could have led to a major fight, but because of Dino's instinct for diplomacy, we just didn't talk to each other for fifteen minutes instead. Finally we found the store.

Actually, I suspect Cathy just claimed to have found the store so Dino wouldn't explode. Wisely, she said she found the item she was looking for but they wanted way too much money for it, and that calmed Dino down.

Because we were so tired of walking, we cruised back to our neighborhood to find a restaurant for our final night in Roma. At the outdoor café il Grillo Brillo, Carolyn did her trick where she makes a couple of beers disappear before we order anything. And once again, the food was great: rigatoni Bolognese, pizza, veal saltimbocca. It would be hard for the other two cities on our agenda to match this.

After dinner, we walked around the Piazza del Monti, looking for a place that sold canoli. This led to the back end of a nice companion piece to the Dino language issue on the bus from the Colloseum on our first day. On that first day, he couldn't get the bus driver to understand "Colosseum" after I quickly and efficiently got us on the wrong bus. Now on our last evening, we were in a little café for desert. Dino wanted a canoli but couldn't find anybody who understood the word. I started thinking that maybe canoli weren't Italian but perhaps Greek. Finally a man sitting along the wall of the café reading a paper got up and said, "Ganoli!" and the baker and the counterperson said, "Oh, ganoli, ganoli! … No we don't have them." Dino cursed them out, and we left with none of us getting desert. *That* wouldn't happen again.

Carolyn wanted to walk around some more and had already forgotten what happened less than three hours earlier, so we ended up on some generic city street with business buildings and no sights of interest. But we were lost, so we had that going for us. Eventually we got back to the hotel and packed it in for the night. Dino sat alone on his balcony, sobbing gently for Mario. Rome had far exceeded our expectations, but the only ideas I had for the book were colorful trash and the healing power of cannelloni. It wasn't much, but it sounded fresh and creative. All I needed was to find another 200 pages worth of ideas in Florence and Venice and I was set.

September 14: According to Dino

It's Sunday morning, and that means Cathy and I sleep in. The Grecos are up early and go to church, which really pisses me off. Look, I already realize that I'm going to hell, but who needs to be constantly reminded? My wife assures me that she is not going to hell, because everything she does wrong is my fault, and God knows this. I doubt that she's right. I mean, God's a busy guy, and he can't possibly keep up with all of the crap that I do. Plus, he's really into forgiveness, and God knows (excuse the pun) that I keep him pretty busy in that department. So I *try* to convince my wife that we should really go to church (never know if God's reading this). And she *flatly* refuses, so I have no option but to get up late and accompany her on a stroll through town.

After about fifteen minutes we find ourselves at a piazza crowded with locals selling stuff on foldout tables. As Cathy shops (really?) I casually amble into a little coffee shop on the square. I ask for an espresso in Italian and throw down a few Euros and leave it there because I can't understand what the owner says when he tells me how much it costs. I sit down and open an Italian newspaper and chuckle as if something I've read is amusing, then practice a few Italian facial expressions that my grandfather used to make. I take another sip of my espresso. I'm sure I've got the old Italian guys sitting around me fooled when Cathy walks in, asking me what the hell I'm doing. I sulk out after her.

The Grecos meet us, babbling about how they walked down Via Greco, made a left on Strada di Greco and saw a building with a plaque on it that said, Greco. I tell them that I had a similar experience. On the way to the piazza this morning, I looked down and realized that I had stepped in some dog Greco.

Cathy, Pete, and Carolyn are getting bummed because this is our last day in Roma, and I'm feeling it too. We jump into the *correct* bus and head over to some sights we want to see before we leave. We head to the Mouth of Truth. Many people know it from the famous scene in the movie *Roman Holiday* where Gregory Peck pulls out his empty sleeve from the open mouth of the stone face and Audrey Hepburn flips out. You can't tell from the movie, but it's actually located in an area along the side of a little church. We have to wait in a line to see the Mouth of Truth, and a vendor has set up a stand nearby where he sells little handmade flutes. Business is good because all of the tourists are posing for photos by sticking every appendage possible, without getting arrested, into the Mouth, while the line barely moves. Pete buys a flute for himself and for a little Italian kid who is really amazed that an American guy would buy him something that his mother clearly wasn't about to. It was a nice gesture, and I was really impressed that Pete would do that. The flute cost five Euros, so I reached in my pocket and slipped the kid six. Never know if God's watching. Like the old joke, I don't have to outrun the bear, just Pete.

So I'm feeling pretty good about myself and the slick way I out-good-deeded Peter. I take pictures of the Grecos sticking their own appendages into the Mouth (and Nose) of Truth, and then when it was our turn I take advantage of the situation. When Cathy puts her hand into the mouth, I ask her about some good looking guy she used to know before we were married. She had always maintained that nothing had happened between them. So I ask her again, and she repeats the same bullshit story. She pulls her arm out, and her hand is still attached. So much for the Mouth of Truth.

A couple hundred yards away is Circus Maximus. I love the way that sounds, especially the way the Romans say it in the movies. You ever wonder why Romans always have English accents in the movies? It's like the world assumes that Americans are so stupid that any European accent is interchangeable. If you ask me, it would be a lot more logical if they all talked like Tony Soprano (but without the speech impediment). Anyway, Circus Maximus is where they held the chariot races, and I'm expecting this big deal like something out of *Ben Hur*. But it's just a flat field with a gravel track that's worn into the grass. That's it. Looks like a Mexican soccer field. A real letdown but I have this sneaking suspicion that Carolyn is trying to pass off this empty lot as the Circus Maximus because she can't find it. I can't be sure though so I take a few pictures just in case.

Across the street is the Temple of Vesta, a small, circular building with evenly spaced columns all around it and a beautiful fountain a few yards away. To me, this is the best part of Rome. It isn't just the major attractions that you already know about; it's the hundreds of ancient structures that are everywhere you look. There's something especially unique in seeing a modern bus pull in front of a structure thousands of years old. Again, that combination of ancient and modern is fascinating. You get the sense that one of them is anachronistic but you can't tell which is which.

That night we leave the hotel and head to my favorite thing, dinner. Nowhere in mind, but that never matters, so we stop at the first outdoor trattoria that looks interesting. In this case, it's supposed to be outdoors. Somehow that makes a difference. We *mangia* like there's no *domani*. Then, when the dessert comes, I pull out something I've bought that I think trumps every "Greco" name reference Pete keeps throwing in my face. It's a coffee cup with the outstretched finger of God almost touching the finger of Adam, the one that Michelangelo painted in the center of the Sistine Chapel ceiling, and in Italian it says, "Creatzione di Adamo." The creation of Adam. Pete says it's not spelled the same. Screw him. I still have the cup.

That night after dinner, we decide to take a break from gelato and look for pastry. While the others are milling about, I go into a wine shop where an old American lady is making a scene, telling the owner that she's extremely angry, and besides that, what he's doing is illegal. It seems she saw a bottle of Australian wine on a shelf, and it's the same bottle she brought to the owner a few days earlier as a gift. This gives new meaning to the concept of re-gifting, but she keeps going on and on about it until I'm about *quattro momento* from throwing her out myself. The manager keeps saying in Italian that he doesn't understand what she's saying, and she finally gives up and leaves. I ask the guy where I can find a pastry place in *vincino*. In perfect English, he directs me to a place around the corner.

When I find the shop I go inside and ask the girl in the front, "Scuzi, ma avette canoli?" She looks like I've asked if they have Mets jerseys in stock. I keep repeating the same thing until finally one man looks at me and says, you mean canoli? Now I'm pissed. It's like the Colosseum thing. So I politely ask if they understand *vaffanculo*? I think they did.

The Coliseum: Construction was begun in 72 AD and finished in 80 AD. It was last used over twelve hundred years ago, for a Rolling Stones concert, I believe.

Circus Maximus in Rome is not quite the draw it was back in the day. This is where they also held Boat show Maximus and Dog Show Maximus. Evidently it is now Jogging Trail Maximus.

Raphael's "School of Athens" Painted in the Palace of the Vatican in 1511. It depicts great figures of Greek thought like Socrates. Our tour guide claimed the fresco also included images of Abraham Lincoln, Yogi Berra, and Captain James Tiberius Kirk.

My $11 camera was of absolutely no value unless we were in the middle of an open field at high noon. Everything looked like a Moody Blues Album Cover. For example this is the ceiling of the Sistine Chapel...or a bowl of fettuccini carbonara...

Part 3: Florence: Climb the Duomo?
You take the steps, I'll take a nap

Monday, September 15: Peter's Version

After a little breakfast, we took a cab to the Stazione Termini for the train ride to Florence. The redcap wanted forty-five Euros to take our bags to the right track. Dino negotiated with him for a couple of minutes, and so we ended up paying about fifty Euros. Each train car had rows of seats that faced each other. We were in car nine, seats thirteen, forty, fifty-six, and seventy eight—which were somehow all in the same row. Go figure. I asked Dino and Cathy if they wanted to sit next to each other. They both looked at me as if I'd asked them if they wanted to try to jump off the train when it hit top speed. I sat across from Dino on one side of the aisle, and Cathy and Carolyn sat across from each other across the aisle. It was a great train ride with a view of some nice countryside and various neighborhoods.

Right on time, we arrived at the Florence train station, and I immediately had a good feeling about the place. We gathered the bags and headed outside to get in line for a cab to the hotel. While in line, I looked across the street and saw Charlie Watts, the drummer for the Rolling Stones, casually strolling along with a camera around his neck. There was no doubt who he was. I mentioned it to the rest of the gang. Carolyn asked if I should go up and say something. I knew that if I did, it would come out something like, "Charlie Watts, I can't believe you're here. This is amazing. I love the Rolling Stones, not as much as the Beatles, and I never thought your drumming was anything special, but it's still so cool to see you. Why did Mick Taylor quit the band, and what is that stuff Keith has caught in his hair? I say it's a fishing lure, my buddy thinks it's a Christmas decoration ..." By that time the police would have arrived and taken me into custody, so I passed. But Dino was nice enough to yell, "Yo, Charlie," to see if he reacted. After forty years of concerts, Charlie Watts' hearing is probably at a point where anything short of a building collapse is background noise. He just kept walking.

Our driver's cab apparently had some sort of malfunction, because she was unable to drive with all four tires on the road at the same time. The ride took only five minutes, and I tried to figure out the route so we could find the station later, but I was being thrown around the inside of the cab so badly that when I was able to look out the window, all I could see was the sky, the street, or a terrified pedestrian.

The signature site of Florence is il Duomo, the dome on the cathedral of Santa Maria del Fiore. It is in the heart of Florence and Cathy arranged for us to stay at Il Solato de Firenze, right around the corner from the cathedral and close to almost everything we wanted to see in Florence. The hotel building housed two floors of hotel rooms, several small businesses, and apartments. The only small knock on the place was that while we were there, it was undergoing some exterior renovations, so there was construction noise. Plus our room had scaffolding and protective mesh outside the window. Fortunately, Dino and Cathy didn't have scaffolding outside their window, which would have ruined the effect *of their balcony*. Now, I could have gone on the offensive about balcony equity, but Dino would have been able to counter with Cathy's arranging the whole trip versus Carolyn's arranging a bozo Vatican tour guide, so it was better to let it go.

The owner/manager was a young man named Enzo. This facility was more security conscious than the Hotel Artorius, or Fort Knox. A large outside door required an electronic key, then there was a second door that opened automatically, and a wide stairway leading to the second floor. On the second floor, a traditional key unlocked a door; through that door there were guest rooms on the right and a breakfast room on the left. So now Dino and I each had three keys in our hands. While Enzo was explaining them, Dino got that expression on his face that said, "I'm only pretending to pay attention. Pete, better get all of this, because I'm blaming you no matter how badly I screw up these fucking keys." When Enzo was done explaining the keys and the security system, Dino said, "OK, so which one opens up my room?" Enzo pointed to a key, and Dino was done.

Our rooms were near the office and the breakfast room, which had BBC news on all day. I was shocked and disappointed to find that the BBC did not cover Major League Baseball's National League Eastern Division pennant race. (I hadn't yet figured out how to get baseball scores from my BlackBerry.)

The train ride from Rome took a little more than two hours and we were ready to stretch our legs a little bit, so we got out the maps and found our way to the Mercato Centrale, the outdoor market where people sold everything from pasta, to ties, to luggage, and almost everything in between. Unlike some of the flea markets we've been to at home, this one had only a small percentage of genuine crap, and even that was disguised pretty well. The transformation that Cathy and Carolyn underwent when they saw the market was scary. Normally, they have pleasant, easy-going expressions on their faces. When we turned the corner and saw all of the stalls and storefronts, their whole demeanor changed. They were like superheroes spotting a crime. The smiles disappeared. Their postures stiffened into a battle-ready stance. They quickly reconnoitered the scene, making hundreds of calculations instantaneously, such as where to make their first assault, and casualty projections (i.e., how much flak Dino would give them). Without exchanging so much as a word or a glance, they moved in at the same time toward the same stall. We would split up several times during the operation, but their shopping sisterhood radar brought them back together at regular intervals. Dino and I were the equivalent of the quartermaster corps. We were there to hold bags, offer largely ignored opinions, and get things down from high shelves.

This all lasted two hours, but to Dino and me, it seemed like forever. For Cathy, it was like a good stretch before a workout. I'll tell you how good this market was: I stayed and shopped for two hours, even though there were no baked goods involved. After about three or four aisles, we had a good idea of what was being sold and could start bargain hunting. Dino was negotiating pretty actively and got a fellow to sell him a tie with an eight-euro price tag on it for six Euros. All Dino had to do was buy a second eight-euro tie for eleven Euros. We finally got through to the other side of the market with about six shopping bags. Cathy was happy and relaxed. I almost expected her to start smoking a cigarette.

We left the market and casually strolled back to the hotel, taking note of some of the landmarks and places we wanted to see later. Florence is smaller and a little more compact than Rome, and most of the streets lead to something that can be used as a landmark, so we got a better feel more quickly. I would say I only led us past the same things three times before finding the hotel, unlike the seven or eight times we saw the same buildings on the first day in Rome. Back at the hotel, Dino got some restaurant recommendations from Enzo. He warned Enzo not to screw up dinner for us—and he didn't smile when he said it. Cathy told Enzo that it was useless to try to win Dino over; his heart belonged to Mario. The recommendation for this first night was a place called Marione (according to Dino this translated to "Big Mario"). Enzo told Dino that we should get there a couple of minutes before 7, when the doors opened, and just find a seat. It sounded a little suspicious, but I figured the guy was too scared to steer Dino wrong.

While Dino and Cathy unpacked and relaxed, we set out to find where our daughter Jackie was staying. Although we were on unfamiliar turf, it took us only fifteen minutes to get to her apartment building, which was around the corner from the main classroom facility. We had forgotten that Jackie told us she would be in class at the time we wandered by, and we weren't sure if her apartment was on the sixth or seventh floor. This being a beautiful, classic Florentine building, it had no elevator. Two five-step stairways separated each floor, and we went all the way to the seventh floor, knocking at each of the two doors on the sixth and seventh floors, but got no answer. By the time we got back down to street level, my thighs were burning like a football player's during the first spring practice—from what I've read. We leisurely strolled back to the hotel, unpacked, and flopped for a couple of hours.

At about five-thirty, we sent Jackie a text message, and she replied that she was "home". We were walking, slowly, down her street when suddenly we heard her yell, "Mom!" from the sixth-floor window. Hearing her baby (albeit a twenty-one-year-old baby) daughter's voice, Carolyn cried, "Jackie!" and for the only time in our life together, Carolyn took off at a dead run, leaving me in her wake. She got to the building, threw open the door, and started running up the stairs, downshifting to a trot by the third floor. She slowed to an enthusiastic stride by the fourth, and by the fifth floor she was clinging to the banister, yelling for Jackie to come and get her. The two of them hugged in the stairwell while I made my way up. Jackie invited us to see the apartment, and Carolyn quickly said yes, I offered to stay put and keep an eye on the stairs while they hiked the rest of way up to the apartment, but that plan was scotched. Her place was sprawling, with two levels and a little window nook in the kitchen from where you could see the Duomo. It wasn't fancy, but it was comfortable and safe. We felt reassured seeing where she would be staying for the next four months—and knowing that we would never have to walk up those stairs again.

Jackie was doing great. Even though she was still homesick and missed her boyfriend, she was beginning to appreciate what a fantastic city she was living in and enjoying her new roommates. Compared to me, when it comes to being adventurous, Jackie is Marco Polo. I wouldn't have considered going to a foreign country for school. I didn't even leave the state. She had only been in Florence for two weeks but had already found a secret bakery that sold items out of the back door at 4 a.m.—about the time she was wrapping up her evening. This place evidently made baked goods for restaurants and cafes in the neighborhood, but would sell retail out of its back door if you knew when and where to go. She'd also made friends with Carlo, who owned a leather-goods shop, and she'd begun negotiating on a leather coat. This would be a semester-long project. Her goal was to get him to give it to her as a going away present, but short of that, she would accept a price cut from $650 to $200. (She got it.) She had trips planned to Ireland, Nice, and southern Italy. Some of her roommates were going to visit Amsterdam, but Jackie said she wasn't sufficiently into smoking weed to join them. Carolyn and I were proud of the way our jaws didn't drop when she told us that.

Carolyn, Jackie, and I walked around her neighborhood and then found our way down to Marione. We got there early, and Dino and Cathy joined us a short time later. We looked in the window and saw the staff eating dinner. The door was locked. It felt a little bit like watching feeding time at the zoo.

At 7 p.m. they opened the doors. We were near the front of the line and found a table near the front of the restaurant. There was no need to go looking for anything with more atmosphere. Giant hams of all kinds were hanging along the walls. At first I figured they were decorations, like at Italian restaurants and delis at home—until one of the employees took one down and cut a few slabs off for a customer getting a take-out order. Somewhere a U.S. FDA inspector was having a stroke.

The tables were crammed together. Normally that would be a turnoff, but we got to see what other people were ordering, and it was so appetizing, nobody minded. A couple of ladies sitting next to us got a plate of sliced meats for an antipasto. They were beautiful—not the ladies, the food. As a matter of fact, the women could have been on fire and I wouldn't have noticed, except to maybe toast my bread before putting a piece of salami on it. I started sending psychic messages to them to offer us a bite, but nothing doing.

We had tortellini Bolognese, osso buco, ravioli, chicken, and lots of wine. The food was so good we would just look at each other and say "… do you believe … how … can't finish thought … food too good …" We actually got tired from raving about it, and the last fifteen minutes of eating were silent, except for a couple of moans and sighs. I realize that sounds almost pornographic. So be it; the food was that good.

After dinner we walked Jackie back to her place, and then the four of us went walking through Florence. It got a little chilly, but as we approached the Piazza della Republica, or Democratica, or Independica, we started hearing music from some sort of flute. By this time it was pretty dark, and we came to a narrow street at the bottom of the steps to a grand building. There, a well-dressed man was playing the music, aided by a microphone and a small amplifier. Dino was convinced the guy was flute-synching to a CD. He had a point. The fellow was doing all this dramatic posing and not missing a note. All this was nice, but it really only served to fill the time between dinner and desert. Tonight we took a break from the usual gelato—and got a waffle with gelato on top. It was a daring leap of extravagance, but we were rewarded. It was our first visit to a Grom, part of a chain of gelaterias throughout Italy. We walked a little more and then decided to turn in.

With about seven days left until I was to meet with the literary agent, I spent about an hour pouring over my notes. Maybe what I had was the makings of a humorous Italian Restaurant Guide. We had certainly been to a bunch of restaurants. I could do some funny stuff on ordering with the wait staff and the language barrier. I was always finding myself caught between trying to pronounce the Italian words with a strong accent and just blurting them out in my flat American dialect. Usually I started strong and halfway through ordering something I would lose my nerve. At that point the server would say, "So you want the chicken or what?" Dino on the other hand pronounced everything with authentic gusto. After which the server would say, "I'm sorry, we're not serving shoelaces tonight, why don't you have the chicken like your friend here?" This had the makings of a decent idea. I could incorporate the food review with amusing little vignettes about each place. This was even better than the lady meeting a dog and eating ice cream.

We were going to spend the next day getting a good feel for the city, but there was one little housekeeping task we had to address.

September 15: According to Dino

We get to the train station, and a porter meets the cab with a cart for the luggage. The whole trip I always make a point of asking everyone, "Quanto costa?" so I don't get ripped off. And every time I do, I feel like a cheap shit, because when they tell me how much it is, it's always reasonable. So this one time I let my guard down and let the guy take the luggage. And it costs me fifty bucks for him to roll the bags thirty yards. Son of a bitch. This guy must have a house next to George Clooney on Lake Como, but probably bigger, because unlike him, Clooney has to pay taxes. We wait about forty minutes until the train arrives, and we have to get all the bags onboard. So we each take some, but Cathy has a bad back, so I make sure she only takes half her luggage. I keep my eye on the rest until she comes back for the other half. Gotta be careful with a bad back.

While we're on the train to Firenze, I have our luggage under constant surveillance, making sure none of it gets ripped off. I almost tackle an old Italian lady who I think has grabbed one of our things, but it looks more like one of the Grecos' bags, so I let her go. Luckily (for them) it isn't theirs, and everything we all start with we actually end up with.

Sitting next to me is a young Italian girl, maybe twenty-two or so, who is reading an Italian Donald Duck comic book. I start talking to her in Italian and am able to communicate fairly well, considering that she speaks almost no English. She tells me she went to America once but couldn't buy Disney comics there. I try to tell her that's impossible because that's where Disney started, but when I get back home I find out she is right. In Italy, Disney comics are very big, but not only are they hard to find in the U.S., the cartoon artwork in the American version is in a new style that looks like shit, and the whole thing is about ten pages. What the hell is that all about? Is nothing sacred? Anyway, she gives me her comic when she is done, and I tell her "Grazie mille." I look at a couple of the pages, sit back, and close my eyes, and in my relaxed mind I start thinking of something that's been nagging me for the last few days. I am almost asleep when I finally get it. It is the only other thing we had asked Carolyn to take care of in Rome. She was supposed to get us to the Piazza Navona, where Bernini's famous Fountain of the Four Rivers is. That was it! Now ask me why we don't have any pictures of it. Answer: *Because we never went there!*

Firenze is unlike Roma because it's smaller and is more of a medieval city rather than an ancient city. It has a lot of college kids and a cool, younger vibe. The little hotel that Cathy booked is right in the middle of things, right around the corner from the Duomo, which is a huge, beautifully ornate church and the centerpiece of the city. The hotel's a nice place, clean and warm, with a TV and books in the room where you get your *colazione* (breakfast) each morning. The owner is a young guy, Enzo, who rented space in an office building and turned it into a small hotel. I love it when young people try entrepreneurial things and work hard at it. We're a little beat from the trip, but after we unpack, we talk to Enzo about sights and restaurants *in vicino*. Enzo has a different approach from Mario. When you asked Mario a question, actually any question, he would say, "Ima no sure." I mean it. Any question. Enzo, on the other hand, always has an answer. It takes us a few days to figure out that none of the answers are right.

Dino: "Enzo, what time does such and such open up?"

Enzo (no hesitation): "Ten a.m."

Dino: "Do we have to get there early?"

Enzo: "No. No problem I think."

Reality: Such and such opens at eight, and when we get there at ten, the line is five kilometers long. (Unfortunately, I don't know how long a kilometer is, and I get in the damn line).

Pete and Carolyn go off to find their daughter, Jackie, who's living in Florence wasting her parents' money—I mean studying, which allows Cathy and me to have some time to our selves. After unpacking, I'm ready to take a walk, but Cathy has this preoccupation with wanting me to get a colon inspection ever since she saw a special on TV just before we left for Italy. So she tells me this is a good time to call the U.S. and schedule an appointment. I tell her I'll do it when I get back, but it's like when she tells me to take out the garbage. If I don't do it the minute she tells me to, she gets pissed. The garbage guys won't even turn down my street for twelve hours, so what freaking difference does it make if I take it out then or thirty minutes later? Women are very weird this way.

This is one of those battles that I know I can't win (which is eerily similar to every other battle I'm engaged in with her) so I call home and my son gives me the doctor's number. I say thank you and so does AT&T, because it just cost me twenty bucks. I then call the doctor's office, and a duty nurse says in a robot-with-an-attitude voice, "What procedure are you trying to schedule?" I try to explain, but she cuts me off and asks me the same question again. I don't know the name of it, and I don't like her attitude, so I tell her I want a "scopeupmyasscopy." She says, "What?" I tell her again, and click, she hangs up. Another twenty bucks. I call again, get the same nurse. I tell her I want to schedule a "scopeupmyasscopy." Click. Twenty bucks. Finally I just schedule an upper GI. I don't know what the hell an upper GI is, and I probably don't need an upper GI, but I can't afford any more phone calls. I tell Cathy that I got the appointment. She looks happy.

We take a walk around town, and Cathy is in heaven because there's a gelato store every ten feet. Unfortunately, every twenty feet you see a group of Albanian gypsies. You know they're Albanian gypsies because they are the only ones who look like homeless New Jersey Teamsters. They have this operation going. They scatter a bunch of art prints on the sidewalk, and they berate you to buy something if you so much as glance at one of them. A real pain in the ass, but I win because they only *look* like they're from New Jersey. I, on the other hand, was freaking *born and raised* in New Jersey. They didn't have a chance. I start to have some fun with them. I look at Cathy and say, "Oh look, honey, wouldn't this look good over the couch next to the picture of the nun?" Then I ask the nearest gypsy how much, and I say, "Wow, that's a good price."

Screw them.

I'm starving, and we're first in line at a restaurant called Marione. Since the door is locked, we're all reduced to standing there like a bunch of homeless New Jersey teamsters, pathetically staring at the staff through the window as they eat. It is pretty obvious that they could care less that thirty customers are staring at them, drooling, as they slowly twirl their spaghetti, oblivious to anything except what's on their plate. They take their time finishing every last morsel, and only when they're absolutely ready do they unlock the doors. The waiter turns the dead bolt and yanks the door, at which time the entire crowd surges forward. The door doesn't open. The waiter smiles and pulls the door and the crowd surges again. Door's still closed. By this time I'm being crushed against the damn door. The waiter smiles again and I mouth to him that if this freaking door doesn't open this time I'm going to kill him. Not sure if he understood me or just got tired of the game but the door suddenly swings open and everyone rushes in like starving cattle. I think I'm pretty slick and pick a table for two, but when I look up I see that Cathy and the Grecos, now three of them including Jackie (they multiply so quickly, just like Irish people), are already sitting at another table with an empty chair. As I join them, Carolyn grins and points to a cash register that says "Greco" on it. It's gonna be a long night. As I take my seat. I quickly try to change the subject and remember that Cathy told me earlier in the day that Carolyn told her that Pete was writing a book about Italy and he's starting to freak out because he's got to meet some guy in Venice and so far he's got squat. Evidently Pete didn't want Carolyn to tell Cathy because she might tell me and "you know how Dino can be". I have no idea what they are talking about but I'm just getting ready to rub it in and ask Pete how the book is coming when the waiter comes over and looks at me. Slight dilemma. Should I try to make Pete feel even worse than he does, or order dinner? No contest. I get tortellini bolognese, and it's the best thing I've ever eaten (sorry, Grandma) in my life. Pete gets the same thing, and after the first bite, he's banging the top of the table like Fred Flintstone. The place is exactly how you'd picture a small neighborhood *ristorante* in Italy, with cheeses and salamis hanging from the ceilings. The *vino di casa* is nice and dry, but unlike many dry wines, it has a full fruity flavor (say that three times fast). The Grecos and Cathy are loving everything as much as I am. Another great thing about the Italians is that they make dinner an all-night affair. The waiters don't try to rush you and flip the tables. You can stay there as long as you want with no nasty stares. Also, the tips are usually included. My kinda country.

On the way home, we walk through one of the most famous piazzas; the Piazza della Signoria, which is filled with about a dozen large concrete statues. A version of Michelangelo's *David* is there; good, but definitely not like the original. Cellini's bronze statue *Perseus* shows the mythic Greek hero holding up the severed head of Medusa. My favorite is Giambologna's *Rape of the Sabine Women*. It shows a younger man holding a struggling naked woman as he stands over a vanquished older warrior. Carpe Diem, or in this case, Carpe la Donna (Seize the Woman). Believe it or not, this thing is actually getting me excited, which is, by the way, the first time I've come close to getting a woody by looking at a four-hundred-year-old carved block of marble. And of course you just can't find an Italian piazza without a fountain in it, and the one here is called Fontana di Nettuno. It commemorates the sea god Neptune. Now I know why the Romans had so many Gods - so they could name all of their fountains.

By now it's pretty dark, and just off the square, alongside the Uffizi Gallery, a crowd of people is gathered around a guy playing a flute. The acoustics are great, but I can see the little boom box that supposedly is only accompanying him with background music. We're supposed to believe that the guy is providing the "live" flute music but my New Jersey instincts are telling me that this is bullshit. Everybody in the crowd is oohing and ahhing, thinking this guy is amazing. I'm just trying to figure out how I can get around them and kick the CD player, but then I think, what the hell? If he can get away with it, so can I. People are dropping tips into his empty flute case like crazy, and I make a mental note to tell Cathy to buy a CD, as I intend to lip-synch my ass off one night when there's no moon out. The next day she buys Gladys Knight, which I think I can pull off, but Pete, Carolyn, and Cathy absolutely refuse to play the Pips. I don't care. I'll hire three Albanians.

Tuesday, September 16: Peter's Version

Although we packed a lot of clothes for this trip, after a full week it was getting close to funky time for a few items. We asked Enzo about laundry service, and he told us of several Laundromats in the area. Later we found out the hotel had a laundry service, but Enzo just didn't want any of my clothes in his machines. We decided to bundle up our respective washes and headed out. It took Dino and I about ten seconds after breakfast to identify the items we wanted washed. For a guy it's an easy call, and I don't think I need to go into detail as to why. So Dino and I waited in the lobby area outside our two rooms for Cathy and Carolyn to come out with the laundry. Most women have trouble deciding what they want to wear. Carolyn has trouble figuring out what she wants to wash. Cathy came out with the D'Adamo laundry, and the three of us waited for Carolyn. Dino asked, "Where's Carolyn?" I looked around the lobby and then pointed to our room and said, "I'll bet she's in there." Two minutes later, Carolyn emerged happily with the laundry.

The Laundromats in Florence were almost exactly like those at home. We found a few vacant washers and loaded them up. Without a TV featuring Italian Porn, Dino was going to go nuts waiting for the laundry to get done and would thus be an annoyance to everyone, so I suggested that the other three go for a walk and I would move the laundry along. Everybody agreed with varying degrees of enthusiasm. Cathy, for one had a look of terror on her face and whispered something to Carolyn. Carolyn assured her I was petrified of women's clothing, and the only fear she need have was that I would drop something while moving the clothes from washer to dryer since my eyes would be closed, my head turned away and my hands shaking. At about the same time they were having this conversation, I realized just about the same thing, but with my sunglasses on inside the Laundromat, it was almost impossible to distinguish wet items pulled out in bunches and moved to the dryers. And by the time everything was dry, everybody had returned, and I didn't have to touch any more laundry.

During the dry cycle I took out my trusty note pad and looked over the comments I'd written about the restaurants. We were about 6 days into the trip, and about ten restaurant visits. Even if I stretched things out it was going to be tough to come up with more than 70 pages of hilarious anecdotes and restaurant reviews, not enough to intrigue a literary agent. Plus I realized I would probably have to get permission from all of the restaurants to use their names if I decided to make fun of any aspect of the meal. That would mean contacting them and explaining how I wanted to make fun of their employees in order to amuse Americans. I didn't see me pulling that off very effectively. Another idea shot to hell.

The laundry took us through the morning, and after we dropped off the clothes in our room, we headed down to the Ponte Vecchio. The Ponte Vecchio is one of six bridges over the Arno River in Florence. It was probably originally built during the Roman Era but it was destroyed by a flood and rebuilt in the 14th century. About one and a half car lanes wide, it was built to provide a secure crossing of the Arno River between the Pitti Palace and the Uffizi Gallery for members of the ruling class, with secret rooms and passages built above the street-level crossing. Nowadays it features upscale shops for jewelry, clothes, and accessories, but even if you are only window shopping, the views of Florence alone make it a must.

Carolyn is a pretty good shopper, with the ability to stop on a dime to look at something in a store window. This usually causes a human domino effect, since whoever is behind her never suspects she is about to stop. As good as Carolyn is at shopping, Cathy has her beat hands down. In addition to being a stupendous shopper in her own right, Cathy was looking at store displays to get marketing ideas for her son's girlfriend who was going to design classes in New York. At least that's what she said, and I chose to believe her. Cathy's demeanor changed somewhat when she shopped. For example, normally when she wanted Dino's attention, she would simply say, "Dino." But when she saw something interesting in a store window, she would sweetly say, "Honey?" Dino knew what this meant and usually pretended not to hear Cathy the first time she said it, so Cathy began to say, "Honey? Honey?" Just to get past the initial rebuff. A couple of times it took three "Honeys," a "Dino," another "Honey," and a "Dino, come here!" but eventually Dino realized she wasn't going to stop, and two "Honeys" became sufficient. On rare occasions she sometimes had to say "Honey" twice even when Dino was standing next to her looking in the same window at the same time, because she instinctively knew Dino was looking at sweaters, but dreaming of grappa.

We split up for a few minutes as Carolyn and I went to a store to buy a gift for Cathy for all of the work she had done to make the trip happen. Carolyn found a jacket she thought Cathy would like, and we figured out a way to get it in a bag that wouldn't be obvious. Carolyn was after me to buy something because she knew she would be buying a few things in Florence and she needed something to use as a counter. You see, she knew that inevitably I would complain about all the stuff she was buying, so she needed me to get something so she could say, "Well, what about that shot glass; I didn't say anything when you got that!" It turned out I saw a cool black sweater in a store and went in to find one in my size to try on and get the price. In what would be a recurring theme, they didn't have my size. This was primarily because the sweater I liked so much was a woman's sweater. It was useless trying to ask Carolyn not to tell Dino. Remarkably, he gave me only a couple of shots on that. I think he had so much more material on me that it got lost in the shuffle.

After Ponte Vecchio, we met Jackie at a place that catered to students like her for sandwiches. It was supposed to be like an American hoagie shop. It turns out the only time Italians don't make good food is when they try to make American food. Afterward, Carolyn, Cathy, and Jackie did some window shopping as we headed back toward town. Dino and I spent the time looking into bars and trying to see if we could spot any women not wearing underwear. No luck. And by no luck I mean the only women eschewing undergarments did so only because they clearly had no luck finding anything they liked at Nunzio's Limp and Lumpy Women's Wear.

The Uffizi Gallery is the preeminent center of Art in Florence. The building was originally a Palace for Cosmo de Medici of the powerful ruling family of Florence. It is U-shaped and has four floors of gallery space. Some of the greatest works of art in the world grace its walls. Because of its popularity, visiting isn't done randomly. There are scheduled times throughout the day and you can make a reservation for one of these scheduled sessions. Enzo had made a reservation for us to go to the Gallery for the 5:45 session at the Uffizi, where I got to see my favorite painting, Botticelli's *Birth of Venus*. We also saw the first of Caravaggio's two paintings of Medusa and dozens of other epic works of art. Dino's comment? "Jesus Christ, it's nothing but paintings and sculptures." I think he thought Uffizi was a machine-gun manufacturer, so you can imagine his disappointment. A café on the roof provided great views of the city.

On Enzo's recommendation, we went to a restaurant called Coquararia for dinner. The name is as hard to pronounce as it is to spell. And I think maybe we got it mixed up with some other place with an alphabet-soup name, because this was a bit of a letdown, and I can't believe Enzo would risk disappointing Dino. It was hard to find and very small. There was a long wait, and the food was OK but not great by my new Italian standards. Carolyn ordered pasta with shrimp, but they gave her swordfish and roasted potatoes instead. When Carolyn told them she ordered shrimp and linguini, the server told her they ran out of shrimp and who would eat swordfish over linguini. I might not have a book about restaurants, but the stories kept coming. I mean swordfish and potatoes instead of shrimp and pasta? Don't you need to replace a shellfish with a shellfish? I was going to ask for a ruling but lost interest after the third glass of wine.

That night I started writing in earnest. An idea came to me while I was talking to Jackie about her getting acquainted with Italy. What if *she* had decided to move to Italy permanently instead of just for a semester? Maybe I could make it that her boyfriend broke up with her and she decided she needed a dramatic change of scene to get her life back together. I could incorporate the quirky people and customs I encountered and have them happen to her instead of me. I could work in characters like Mario and John the tour guide. This struck me as a pretty good idea and I got about twenty small pages of it down before going to bed that night. This was a great day.

September 16: According to Dino

When you're in Florence, Italy, the last thing you want to do is spend a morning doing laundry, but by this point we don't have much choice. The previous day we spotted a Laundromat around the corner from Marione and decided to hit it this morning. Luckily I had packed two pair of underwear, but at this point they're both getting a little ripe, and in order to wash both of them, I decide to go commando. I haven't done that in a while, and by the time we get to the Laundromat, I am feeling so damn good that I wonder why I bothered to pack them at all. Could have saved some room in my suitcase and jammed in an extra Rutgers tee shirt. Luckily, there are only a couple of people there, and we load all of our clothes in six washers. I bring a book, figuring this will give me a chance to kick back, but then Pete makes a big deal about not minding staying with the laundry while the rest of us can go out and walk around.

We take him up on it, but I can see that Cathy's acting a little weird so a few minutes later I ask her what's wrong. She tells me she's uncomfortable with Pete handling (translation: fondling) her panties while he puts them in the dryer. My eyes get as big as two cheese raviolis. Son of a bitch. I didn't see that one coming. I immediately turn on my heels and sprint nine blocks back to the Laundromat. The Laundromat was only five blocks away, but I got lost. Did you ever try to maintain a sprint when you know you're lost? It's not easy. Try it sometime.

Anyway, when I get there, Pete is closing the last dryer door, and he turns around with a shit-eating grin on his face. He knows that I know that he knows that I ... whatever. He's got me. Afterward, we can't find one pair of Cathy's panties. The leopard ones, damn it. I shudder to think of what he would do with them when Carolyn goes to sleep. Serves me right for letting my guard down.

My day is already starting on a bad note, but I'm hoping things will get better as we make our way to the Ponte Vecchio. *"Ponte"* means "bridge," and on this famous one that spans the Arno River, jewelry stores line each side of its entire length. Cathy has been in the jewelry business for many years, and she'll admit that the Italian designs and quality are the absolute best in the world, but she tells me that these particular shops are not the top of the line. Nice, but not the best. She still can't resist going into a few of them and ends up buying a nice gold cross for one of our sons.

On the way back to the hotel, we stop at a little shop that faces the river. In the window are framed pictures of beautiful scenes that are totally done in tiny gem stones. They are just mosaics, but the detail is so amazing they could actually be paintings. Cathy and I go inside, and along one wall are workbenches where the scenes are made by hand. On a few of the tables are frames with scenes that are partially finished. Through these works in progress you can see how difficult it must be to create these works of art from miniscule pieces of stone. I find the salesperson and ask her how long it takes for someone to master this art form. She points to an old man leaning over one of the frames and placing a mosaic into place with hands shaking so hard he could be mixing a martini. He must be close to ninety years old, and I can't believe he doesn't send the little rock sailing thirty feet in the air, but he actually gets it exactly where it's supposed to be. I look back at the salesperson, and she says, "Heesa stilla, howa you say? Apprentice." She's gotta be busting my chops, but I'm not completely sure, plus my wife tells me I'm not allowed to make another scene, so I let it go. I know Cathy would love to buy one of these and she's trying to catch my eye but I refuse to make eye contact with her. I figure if it works with the Albanians it should work with her. She's more persistent than the gypsies but I'm not giving in.

Pete strolls into a clothing store and actually considers buying something. This is amazing because Pete never buys anything. He is not a shopper. He's looking at a tight black sweater that would be really popular in the East Village. I'm not sure what he's thinking. Sure, he could tie it around his neck and metro-sexual himself around Florence but what's he going to do when he gets back to Philadelphia. He'd get the shit kicked out of himself... again. Luckily (for him) they don't have his size and we leave.

For lunch we go to an American-style sub shop to meet their daughter, Jackie, again. She's really a cute kid, and we enjoy the time we spend with her. I wait until it's just me, Pete, and Jackie, and say, "Pete, I need a handkerchief. Would you happen to have a handkerchief in your pocket there? Maybe one with leopard spots?" Jackie doesn't know what the hell I'm talking about, but her father's starting to sweat. "What about it, Pete?" Just then Cathy comes over, which lets him off the hook. I eat the rest of my sausage sub, but I keep my eye on him.

When we leave we notice a bride and groom walking together. She's wearing a long, flowing wedding dress that's getting dirty as it drags behind her on the street. Evidently it's a custom in Italy that the bride and groom walk through town. I'm not sure if the custom takes place before or after the wedding, but I assume it's before, because she's not yelling at him yet. It is cool that this is a country that has customs still displayed by people today. Every town and province has their own unique customs and they are very important to the inhabitants. Gives them a connection to their history and their ancestors. Not much of that left in the U.S. First or second generation immigrants had them but now they have almost completely disappeared. A real shame.

That night we hit the Uffizi Gallery, which is next to where the fake flute player set up and where I intend to knock them dead as soon as I can find the right Albanians. The right Albanians defined as ones without beards and with their knives well hidden. You'd think that would be easy to find. You'd be wrong.

The gallery has an amazing collection of different styles of paintings done through different periods of the Renaissance. Works by Botticelli, Raphael, and even da Vinci are on display. Under other circumstances I would have enjoyed it more, but after all the artwork we've been seeing recently, I'm in overload mode, and I find myself staring at a painting while trying to remember the lyrics to *Midnight Train to Georgia*. I glance over at Pete, who looks like a kid in a panty shop as he makes his way from painting to painting, excitedly pointing things out to Carolyn. I, on the other hand, am really getting bored, just going through the motions, wondering when we can get the hell out of here and go eat. Cathy looks like she wants to stay, but I sense that she is getting a little tired too, so I go over to her, feign concern, and say, "You getting tired, honey? "Yeah," she says back, in a voice that sounds like Mona Lisa Vito in the movie *My Cousin Vinny*. I love that movie. I go over to the Grecos and talk low in a sympathetic tone, "I think Cathy's getting tired." Even though they're still really into the museum, they both agree that we'll all leave now and go to dinner. Jerry Callo would be proud.

Pete and I are in the lead as we walk to the restaurant, and he's a little quiet, which is way out of character for Pete. I don't know if this is because he's pissed about leaving the museum early or if he's embarrassed about the little panty incident. Either way, I don't care, because small talk isn't my forte. This turns out to be the first meal we have that none of us raves about. It is good, but definitely not up to the standards we are getting used to. I forgot that Enzo gave me the recommendation and immediately blame the Grecos. They just apologize. The Grecos are really nice people, and sometimes I think they deserve a better friend than I am, but generally I come to my senses pretty quickly. I may not be the perfect friend, but who the hell else are they going to find? Why my hot Asian wife stays married to me is a whole different matter. That's definitely her issue. She has many.

It wasn't until we returned from Italy that I discovered Dino's preoccupation with nude men. I mean, I know it's art, but know when to say when.

Dino called this one "Mario"

Come on, Dino, this guy can't even defend himself

I don't even want to know what he was
thinking when he saw this guy on guy thing

Wednesday, September 17: Peter's Version

The best day yet. Cathy had arranged a day tour with someone named Vincenzo. Many of the tour guides in Italy have full-time jobs and do tours on their days off. This was true of Vincenzo as well. I had a tough time translating what his full-time job was. It was either undercover cop or secretary of state. He asked us not to mention that because it might compromise his viability … as a tour guide.

At first I had doubts about Vincenzo. He said he wasn't allowed to drive in front of our hotel to pick us up because of traffic laws for private cars in Florence. Come on, he's a top government official or a cop; either way, he should be able to drive anywhere. So I pressed the issue until he threatened to deport me for the ugly-ass clothes I was wearing. Now I knew he was legit. First, he took us to the Piazzale Michelangelo, one of the most beautiful man-made sites I've ever seen. It has a vantage point from which you can see just about all of Florence proper—but sadly, no snack bar. Vincenzo took our picture with this vista in the background, and it's one of my favorite pictures from the whole trip. It was early in the day; Dino was still in a good mood.

Then we headed out to the Chianti Classico region of Tuscany, driving through hills of olives and vineyards. Dino was in the front seat, again, and I sat in back with Carolyn and Cathy. Somehow Dino thought he was making out on the deal. Along the way, Vincenzo told us of his various American girlfriends, and that he doesn't like Italian women and they don't like him. He wanted a woman with no makeup and a big chest who was willing to stay home and take care of children. I knew just the woman: her name was Lois, she was 73 years old, and she lived in Palmyra, New Jersey.

Once in the hills of wine country, we stopped at a winery called Vecchio Maggio, where Vincenzo said his sister got married. It was a beautiful place. We had our first wine tasting at 9:30 in the morning. I was trying to calculate what time I should expect the hangover to start, but then they gave us some Vino Santo (holy wine) and we dipped biscotti in it. Screw the hangover, I'm going in. The people of the Vecchio Maggio winery have a feud with the people at our next stop, the Verrazano winery. This is the same family as the man who, Dino said, "Discovered the Verrazano Bridge." Because Verrazano and Vecchio Maggio are on hilltops, you can see each clearly from the other. The Verrazano's family and employees' comment is, "The best thing about Vecchio Maggio is that they get to look at us." Each of these places has a restaurant for meals and special events.

We walked back to the car and headed for Verrazano. I could tell that merely walking was going to take more and more concentration as the day went on. At Verrazano, as we got close to the wine-tasting room, we picked up the aromatic scent of the chef roasting wild pig with rosemary (I was told not to make a joke about the Chef still cooking the pig when Rosemary went home). Even though it was still morning, I could have stopped for dinner right then and there, but if we stopped every time we smelled or saw delicious food in Florence we wouldn't have gone more than five blocks from our hotel.

The third stop was the Fattoria Montagliari. Fattoria can be loosely translated to factory, but in this case the name applied because they produced multiple agricultural items. I liked this smaller place even more than the first two. There was a small vineyard across the dirt road from the main buildings, and about thirty yards into it there was a plum tree. Vincenzo walked us through the building where they stored balsamic vinegar in large casks. It was made of stone and had beautiful, rustic-wood flooring. If you remodeled that building with electricity and plumbing, it would be a $5 million home in southern California. Then Vincenzo took us through the winemaking facility and described the process to us. He said it was all automated now. I think that means there's a light bulb in the grape-pressing room. Vincenzo showed us a device used in the fermentation process that was developed by Leonardo da Vinci that consists largely of a glass tube shaped like an upside-down pear. This tube is inserted into a cask of wine, and the fluid rises and falls in the tube as the wine ferments. That was all I could grasp before Vincenzo's explanation deteriorated into a series of hand gestures and grunts.

The Fattoria made balsamic vinegar, olive oil, honey, and wine. We tasted twenty-six-year-old balsamic vinegar, flavored olive oils, and wine, all of it delicious. I would have paid just for the toast they gave us to dip in the oil and vinegar. A wide variety of items were for sale and Vincenzo doubled as shop clerk. He had to be getting a kickback, right? We bought small bottles of balsamic vinegar and lemon olive oil. Vincenzo told us of a restaurant that had a special dish of steak with a balsamic vinegar and blueberry sauce. I had a tough time with that idea. The owner of the Fattoria, Dave, let us know they had a restaurant that served lunch on the grounds. We would have stayed, but his name was Dave. That kind of ruined it for us. What Italian is named Dave, for God's sake?

After Montagliari, we stopped in the little town of Greve. How many places do you go to for a salami tasting? Wild boar salami, fennel salami, and a few others. Cathy and Dino bought some to bring home. I couldn't imagine even cured meat lasting that long without refrigeration, but later they told us that when they got home, it was still delicious. We bought some nice souvenirs there, including a grappa glass for my buddy Dino. These little towns are the real jewels of Tuscany. There is less tourism, so you can better appreciate the history and natural beauty, as well as get a little insight into daily life. And there are just enough places to pick up local specialty items without feeling pressured or taken advantage of.

Not far from Greve is a beautiful little town called Castellina in Chianti, population seventy. It used to have more residents, but many of the younger people have left for the city, where there are more jobs and a more exciting lifestyle. Built on a hill during the Baroque period in the late sixteenth century, Castellina in Chianti features a walk-through tunnel that runs around the perimeter of the town. The outward facing side of the passageway has portholes about every twenty feet, which were put in so the original inhabitants could look out for invaders, or the pizza guy. The other side of the passageway had small rooms for guards, which were turned into shops. One of the shops sold only leather items, including a golf bag with a matching hat and briefcase. You know typical stuff.

Once outside of the passageway and walking through *the* street (It's a really small town), we saw a little cart from which a lady sold herbs. But the cart was deserted, and a cloth covered its contents. A sign written in Italian hung from the cart. Dino translated the sign as saying, "Please do not touch the cart. I will be back shortly. If anything is missing when I get back, I will shoot you in the ass."

It occurred to me that this could be the ideal place to use as a setting for the book. I could have Jackie find a rundown little apartment or villa that she could fix up. And she could interact with the workers. She could go on a tour with someone like Vincenzo, start to think she likes him and then find out he's married or a cousin. Her friends from home could visit and see how she is starting to act like a native. It could possibly be funny to have a fairly typical 21 year-old American girl become a fairly typical 21 year-old Italian girl. Of course I would need some help figuring what that was, but that shouldn't be too hard. The countryside was beautiful and the people were colorful enough to make it a really cool story. I took note of some of the apartments and villas we passed so I could create a place around which the action would take place.

Vincenzo then drove us to the Etruscan ruins. While it's true I was supposed to do some of the historical research, I admit I had not prepared a dissertation on the Etruscans. First, I didn't know we were going to be visiting any Etruscans, and second had I explained who the Etruscans were, Dino, Cathy, and Carolyn would have looked at me attentively, nodded, and then muttered something about me trying to show off. Besides, I didn't want to steal Vincenzo's limelight. Yeah, that's why I didn't explain about the Etruscans. Turns out he wasn't all that knowledgeable either, but he knew they were dead and pretty short, judging by the height of the underground ruins.

Fortunately, there was a nice view of the countryside, and we didn't stay long. I think we were all getting a little tired of driving, so we stopped at a roadside café in Monteriggione to sober up from the wine tasting and have some lunch. At home I rarely eat lunch and only occasionally eat breakfast, so this stopping for three meals felt strange, but I forced myself to enjoy it. Vincenzo napped in his car while we ate. This place was the equivalent of an American diner, with nothing special from outward appearances. We sat at picnic tables outside. But the food would have embarrassed 80 percent of the Italian restaurants at home. Even the waitress was gulping down a huge platter at the table next to ours when she wasn't serving. When we were done and able to get up (these two events were a good ten minutes apart), we very gently woke Vincenzo, and headed out.

The final stop of the day was Siena. This was the oddest part of the trip in a lot of ways. Much of the city is encircled by a wall. Forty thousand of the city's fifty thousand residents live within the walled portion. The city is divided into seventeen Contrade or wards, each represented by a different mascot. You have your goose, your snail, your caterpillar, your sea shell, your porcupine, and so on. Each district has rules of conduct. They were once very strict but have been relaxed over the years. For example, it is no longer forbidden to eat surf and turf. Before the nineteenth century you couldn't marry outside your district. Now you can marry outside the district as long as you don't have either of the wedding parties' district animals on the menu for the reception dinner.

In addition, twice a year there is a horse race (Palio) run over an oval in the middle of the Piazza del Campo. The oval is made of cobblestones and the Piazza lies within a city square surrounded by older buildings. The 'track" is covered with dirt, and the horses and riders do three laps. Only the horse needs finish. If the rider is thrown, the horse can still win. The riders use whips, called nerbi, which are made from dried and stretched bulls' penises. I can't even say bull penis in my house and these guys get to use them twice a year? The winning district gets to have its flag raised throughout the city and the jockey gets a silk sash (called a palio, thus the name). And that's it. No prize money, no endorsement contracts. A month before we got there, the caterpillar beat the porcupine. Anyway, it sounds like great fun, but I imagine there is a lot of insult trading between contrade. I mean if you're a sea shell, how do you compete with a unicorn or a panther?

Siena is home to the first bank established in Europe; I think it's called the Second National Bank of Italy. A bust of every head of the bank in history protrudes from under the eaves of the building. None of them was smiling. It looked more like a wall of shame. Also in Siena, they prominently display the image of a female wolf being suckled by Romulus and Remus. This includes a sculpture on top of a large base in a major square. That's a little disturbing. But, wait, I haven't even hit the weirdest parts of the day yet.

We headed over to the biggest cathedral in Siena. As in Florence, there was a separate *Battisteria* next to the cathedral, which is where babies are baptized. Vincenzo pointed out that the doors of every Battisteria "are shaped likea boobs, you know boobs?" I acknowledged that I did indeed have a working knowledge of them. He continued, "They shaped likea boobs because theese isa da first place da baby goes without hes a mama, so they want eet to looka familiar." I told Vincenzo that in the U.S. we don't use that term for the female nursing device in polite company. He asked what term we use. I told him we usually say "breast." He said, "'Breast'? ... 'Breasts.' ... No, I like "boobs" betters. Hey, I know another word for them." I put my hand up and told him that would be enough on the topic.

After anatomy class, we walked over to the Basilica San Domenica where the head of Saint Catherine of Siena was displayed. Claiming he'd seen heads before, Dino didn't go in. Inside there are no big arrows pointing to the display case of the head. They don't build it up by having lesser displays like the spleen of Saint Kenny of Chianti. You just walk along the perimeter of the place, and all of a sudden, wham! It looks like one of the Golden Girls without her makeup. Really off-putting. We almost ran out of the place, as if leaving quickly would make the nightmares we were going to have a little less scary.

On the way back to our hotel, Vincenzo made reservations for us at Acqua 2 (pronounced Acqua Due, but written with the 2), the place with the balsamic blueberry sauce on the steak. He said its other specialty was a sampler of five pastas as an appetizer. After relaxing for a while at the hotel, we freshened up and headed over to Acqua 2. Inside it was nicer than a lot of the places we had been to, and we got a nice spot along a half wall where we could see and be seen and also have some elbow room. The menu had fourteen pasta dishes from which five would be served as a *primi piati* (first course). We asked if we could choose which five we wanted. No! OK, then, whatever you say. The five pastas they chose included pasta with broccoli and pasta with red pepper, which I normally would never order. They were all mouthwatering. Cathy was brave enough to order the steak with balsamic vinegar and blueberry sauce. It came out thick, deep purple, and surprisingly good.

After politely tasting wine all day and then sobering up, Dino and I chugged it down with a vengeance at dinner. By the time we were about done eating, we were talking about music, and I started singing Sinatra's version of *The Way You Look Tonight,* and Dino joined in. Then we did *Don't Get Around Much Anymore,* and I think we may even have left our hearts in San Francisco, I can't remember. This was not a little sotto voce half-whispering. We belted them out like we were on stage. We paid the check, got up to leave, and people actually seemed disappointed and asked if we would sing some more. As I said, this was the weirdest day of the entire trip.

After dinner we strolled around and then had tea and desert, and grappa for Dino, at a place called Jilly, which sells everything from pastries, to candy, to coffee and tea, to sandwiches, to cocktails. It has a giant bar and three well-dressed bartenders from whom you order any manner of beverage. Dino managed to piss off all three bartenders in the first two minutes we were there—just a few seconds off his world-record time for simultaneous multiple bartender offending. I forget how he did it, but fortunately the rest of us were able to pretend we weren't with him and got served.

Back at the room after Jilly, we decided to test drive the grappa and Vino Santo we had purchased that day. We also cracked open a bottle of Prosecco that was in the minibar. Cathy, Carolyn, and I reviewed the day while Dino tried to find Italian porn on TV. It was hard for him to channel surf from out on his one-man balcony, but he pulled it off. However, Carolyn and I were asked to leave the room at 1 a.m., because, Dino said, I was bad luck. All he could get on TV were game shows and soccer highlights. The next day he said that the minute I left the room, he hit the jackpot. He was kind enough not to provide details.

September 17: According to Dino

Cathy had found a tour guide who'd gotten good reviews on the Internet, so she reserved him for two days. We meet him in the morning at the corner on the far side of the Piazza del Duomo, which is the closest place to our hotel that allows cars. After making sure he's the right guy through a complicated series of facial expressions, eyebrow calisthenics and head bobs, we exchange greetings and tell him where we want to go that day. He nods and doesn't spit his toothpick out at us, so I assume he is OK with it. His name is Vincenzo, and he is a moonlighting member of the Carabinieri, or national police force. As soon as we start climbing into his small minivan, he starts ogling our women, which I have no problem with, because in my mind, that will serve as his tip. On the other hand, I'm not stupid, so I sit in the front seat with him and let the girls ride in the back with Pete the panty raider. Some choice.

Vincenzo drives like you would think an Italian Carabinieri, or an Italian shopkeeper, or an ... actually, any Italian would. His speed always hovers around ninety to ninety-five miles an hour. The speedometer is in kilometers, but I know the miles conversion because he would say, "Dino, guess how fast we're going right now?" I'd always respond, "I don't know, Vincenzo." And then he would tell me in miles per hour. We had the same conversation every ten minutes.

Vincenzo speaks English really well. He tells us he taught himself by listening to American songs. I, on the other hand, still don't know what "*volare*" means. So I'm trying to talk with him in Italian, for two reasons. First, to brush up on my skills and second to use this as another opportunity to make fun of Pete. I tell Vincenzo that Pete's of indeterminate sexuality, he's not very bright, and he is even older than he looks. Cathy kicks the back of my seat, and I realize the reason I had such an easy time expressing all this was because I was still speaking English.

He drives us further and further into the countryside and soon all we see are vineyards covering every inch of the rolling Tuscan hills. We stop at a few of the vineyards to taste different wines and sample the balsamic vinegars. Up close the vineyards are even more picturesque than they are from a distance. The grounds and old stone buildings blend perfectly into the landscape. Birds are chirping with Italian accents and in the distance dogs are barking. The sights and sounds punctuate the serenity of an old Italian woman intently sweeping grass clippings from ancient stone steps. The broom looks to be as old as she. Here we are led to a back room and see huge wine barrels with ornate glass devices on top of each one. Their purpose is to ensure that the pressure and oxygen levels are kept at just the right levels as the wine ferments. We are told they were invented by Leonardo da Vinci! And no one has been able to improve on them since. Unbelievable.

One of the vineyards we visit was where da Vinci stayed when he painted the *Mona Lisa*. It is beautiful, and I'm sure he enjoyed the built-in pool. We then go to my favorite, the Verrazano Vineyard. Same family as the guy who discovered the Verrazano Bridge. Must have been a hell of a surprise for him seeing that thing in the middle of the wilderness, huh?

We're all really enjoying ourselves, tasting the wines and dipping into various ages of balsamic vinegar with chunks of Italian bread (suppose that's redundant considering where we are). Then Vincenzo pours a clear liquid into small glasses and says it's pure rain water. Nothing like it, he tells us, and says to drink it in one gulp, which we all do, but it's really grappa. I think Cathy and Carolyn are going to pass out. Even though I'm laughing, I'm not sure if Vincenzo is a funny guy or if he's trying to get my wife drunk.

As I said, the vineyards are stunningly beautiful places and the views of the rustic hills are breathtaking. It looks like the place in Sicily where Michael Corleone hid out. It is so serene that I don't want to leave, but I also realized that in a half hour I'd be so bored that I'd want to blow my brains out. So we all get back into Vincenzo's minivan with me riding shotgun (*lupara*).

By this time I'm ready for a little civilization, so we head over to a small town called Greve to taste prosciutto, boar salami, and some other things that taste great but I prefer not knowing where they come from. This is a great little village. There are shops and trattorias surrounding the square where we parked the van, and right in the center of where all of the cars are parked is a huge bronze torso. No arms or legs, but it has a big uncircumcised Greco. Right there in the middle of town. Unbelievable. Vincenzo points it out to my wife and says too bad it has such a small "*sasige.*" Cathy giggles. Giggles! If I had said it, she would have given me a load of shit for being crude. But with Vincenzo, different story. I now have to keep one eye on him and another on Pete. Good thing I don't have to drive.

We then move on to a few other Tuscan towns, each one with its own unique style and charm. After we park and walk through a few of them, Vincenzo stops at a gas station/restaurant on the way to Siena so we can get a quick lunch. We sit at a large picnic table outside and have a nice pasta dish, a thick tubular spaghetti, and of course, a carafe of house wine. The pasta was done perfectly, and remember, this is a freaking gas station. Vincenzo, who was off napping, picks us up when we're done. At least he tells us he was taking a nap. We hope he was, because I think he worked the late shift the night before, and the only thing worse than an Italian driver is a sleep-deprived Italian driver.

Five minutes after leaving, we're on the highway headed to Siena. This turns out to be another great city, not as big as Florence, but much larger than the small towns we have just been to. We park on the edge of the city and take a leisurely tour through a few of the seventeen distinct neighborhoods (*contradas*) that make up Siena, noticing that each one has street signs that mark their territory with pictures of its own particular animal. I'm still looking for the Fried Calamari neighborhood when we come to the square where all the neighborhoods connect, called Piazza del

Campo. This is where they have the famous horse race every six months. Vincenzo tells us a few interesting facts about the race and then says it doesn't matter if a jockey stays on his horse or not. Whichever horse finishes first determines who wins. At this point I'm thinking that if that's the case, then the jockey's just extra weight, so why not just slap the horse on the ass and get out of the way? I'm trying to figure out why it wouldn't work and how I could turn this theory into a few Euros while I follow Vincenzo and the others as they continue their stroll through the plaza. I hear him say that the people in Siena are really nuts (*pazzo*). They identify themselves from a particular neighborhood first, then from Siena, then Italy. Their loyalties are in that order. Real old-school stuff, still alive and thriving right here in the twenty-first century.

The Piazza del Campo is a large wide open space, with a moderate pitch toward the center. People are lying all over the place on blankets, and most are enjoying their lunch as they take food and drink from the wicker baskets they had brought. It looks like Seaside Heights, New Jersey, but without the sand … or the ocean … or the boardwalk. (Actually, I guess it really didn't resemble Seaside at all, but I thought it was about time for another New Jersey reference.)

We move off the square and Vincenzo points out a few more interesting things: the Duomo; the Palazzo Publico, where we see a huge bell tower called Torre del Mangia, some more statues, and a few little parks. We are as interested in the small aspects of the city as we are in the popular sights and there are interesting things to see just about everywhere we look. Eventually we come upon a hill in front of a cathedral where there's a huge bronze statue of running horses. That's where Vincenzo makes his famous "boobs" comment that I hear about later. (I didn't hear it then because I had gone to the bathroom in a little bar on the corner and stopped to stare at the barmaid who had really big boobs. Ironic isn't it?)

On the way back to Florence, we ask Vincenzo if he can recommend a restaurant for dinner that night. While driving, he pulls out his cell phone and calls a place called Acqua Due. He says he only takes dates there if they have a nice rack and he knows he's going to get lucky. I think he shoots another look in the rearview, but I'm not sure because now I'm giggling.

This restaurant is fabulous. We decide on the pasta sampler as the first course for the table, and we ask the waiter if we can pick from the list of the various pastas. He says no, they will bring out the ones they feel like making, but don't worry; we're going to love it, and I'll be damned if he isn't absolutely right. The dishes have sauces that I've never heard of before, including a broccoli sauce and another one made from artichokes. For the main course, Cathy has the reduced blueberry balsamic sauce on a nice tender steak. (Months later she still talks about it. I know, because I heard her telling Vincenzo on the phone the other night.)

Pete and I are pretty loaded, and for some reason he starts singing, low at first, but not for long. Pretty soon I join in, and we're really belting it out. We think we sound pretty damn good, and Pete tells everybody back home that we got a standing ovation. I tell him that generally, standing ovations occur when you finish the song, not twenty minutes later when you're leaving the restaurant. Anyway, we have a ball, and it is another great night.

On the way back to the hotel, we pass a big open bar that sells coffee, liquor, pastries, and chocolates. The first thing you see when you get inside is a big, shiny, old-fashioned brass bar that is about thirty feet long. I'm in a nice mellow mood until I get into it with the bartenders. Here's what happens:

I spot a guy at the other end of the bar who is given a cool-looking drink, and I ask the bartenders what it is. They look at me with a real attitude and tell me I wouldn't understand. I tell them I don't really understand a scotch and water either, but that doesn't stop me from drinking them. I tell them to just give me whatever the hell it is, and they ignore me. Now, normally I'm only ignored by bartenders when I'm half in the bag, which is not the case here, so I am really pissed. I feel like ripping off their bow ties, but then realize it would be meaner to just let them continue to wear them. I am starting to get a real New Jersey thing going and am about two exits away from kicking the shit out of both of them. Thankfully, however, I am able to stop it at the toll booth and force myself to return to my normal sunny disposition.

We head back to the hotel, with Frank and Tony singing on my iPhone while we lounge on the D'Adamo balcony. We crack open some Prosecco and grappa. The Grecos bring munchies and I realize that compared to the waiters, the Grecos aren't half bad. Plus they hardly ever wear bow ties.

Thursday, September 18: Peter's Version

This morning, Dino and I walked from the hotel to the train station to get the tickets for Venice on Monday while Carolyn and Cathy ... didn't. I'm still not sure what they were doing, but I suspect it didn't involve walking twenty blocks. They were probably figuring out what they still hadn't purchased yet. I wanted to walk to the train station so I could figure out, for the book, how easily Jackie could get from Florence to Tuscany by train. This idea was really getting interesting. Jackie's personality lends itself to the story because she's brave enough to try something like a move, but she isn't likely to think about the more obvious complications, like finding a place to live, taking care of it, paying bills, getting to know neighbors. These little details would be the source of some pretty good scenes and lines. I made some quick notes while Dino tried to figure out how to buy the tickets without looking at the directions in English above the ticket window.

When Dino and I got back, we all discussed what we wanted to do that day. Carolyn and I wanted to try to climb the four hundred and fifty steps to the top of the famous Duomo at the Cathedral Santa Maria de Fiore. I asked Dino if he wanted to come with us. He said, "Climb the Duomo? Are you fucking crazy? If I wanted to work that hard I would have stayed home and mowed the fucking Rose Bowl. I'll tell you what, you climb the steps, I'll take a fucking nap." So we decided we would tour the town separately for a chunk of the day and then try to meet up to see the statue of David later in the afternoon. As much as we were enjoying each other's company, I think getting a chance to do some things separately and catch up as a couple was good to do, too. Dino seemed happier about it than anybody.

So Carolyn and I went to il Duomo. The line wasn't long, and we were quickly going up the steps. We couldn't believe there was even artwork to look at along the stairway throughout the walk to the top of the Duomo ... and again, no freaking snack bar. The steps are about three feet wide, and there is no extra room except for a little space every 150 steps where you can just about turn around. I am not sure I figured out exactly how the steps worked, but I think the "up" stairs went clockwise wrapping around the dome from the east to the south, and the stairs heading down wrapped around clockwise from the south to the west. However, nobody follows the directions, so we had people of every nation trying to wedge past us going down the up staircase. When we finally got to the top and stepped outside and saw the entire city beneath us, we said to ourselves, "God Almighty, I gotta walk all the way down those stairs again?!" The view was spectacular, but we couldn't help speculating about what Dino would say if he was up there with us. We settled on, "Nice spot. There better be an elevator or a grappa salesmen up here, or somebody's in trouble, Petey." We could see Jackie's apartment building between us and the train station. I actually started getting sentimental about the idea of her really moving to Italy permanently and how much I would miss her.

We managed to get down the stairs easier than up, primarily because people weren't going up the down stairs as much as they were going down the ups. After recovering from the descent, we got a sandwich and looked over the list of things we had planned to do while in Florence. There were only two things left: Boboli Gardens and the *David* at the Galleria Academia. Because we were going to try to meet Dino and Cathy to see the *David* together, we headed to the Boboli Gardens, which are across the Ponte Vecchio.

I should point out that it took us most of the morning to get used to not having Dino around. Every time one of us said something we would pause, expecting Dino to comment. When it didn't happen, we almost forgot what we had originally said. Carolyn said, "Funny how you can get used to something like that after only a month." I told her it had only been a week. "Not in Dino years," she replied. I wondered out loud if Dino and Cathy were having trouble getting used to us not being around. Carolyn felt Dino probably hadn't even realized we weren't there yet. Or else he was trying to figure out why he was in such a good mood.

The Boboli Gardens, located behind the Pitti Palace, were built in the mid-sixteenth century by the Medici family. With an amphitheater, rose garden and porcelain museum, Boboli is an expansive and meticulously landscaped haven. At the highest point you get beautiful views of Florence and the surrounding Tuscan countryside. We spent most of the afternoon there and I don't think we covered 75% of the property. The centerpiece is a beautiful, ornate fountain surrounded by a large pool with fish and swimming birds. It had buildings that no longer had any real function but were maintained beautifully. The Porcelain Museum had a display of dishes and other dining pieces from the seventeenth and eighteenth centuries. I'm a semi-typical guy and I was really impressed so you can imagine what somebody with a genuine artistic sense would feel about this place. Near the rose garden there is a water fountain. The water spurts from the mouth of a brass angel set in at the bottom of the fountain's bowl. It was when I was taking pictures of the water fountain that I realized how strangely normal and almost boring it was without Cathy and Dino. Damn it, he had raised the entertainment bar for the trip, and now it was dipping without him. I knew this could happen before we decided to go, but I had assumed he would have pissed me off so often by this point that I would have been glad to get rid of him for a while. I actually thought Cathy would have gotten pissed off at him too by this point, and the three of us would have gone to a formal tea or maybe a picnic by a river. But no, he had been pretty enjoyable, even while being Dino. This was totally unanticipated, and I had no remedy. We would have to stick out the rest of the afternoon by ourselves as best we could and hope we didn't seem too anxious when we saw them again.

Just then, Dino texted us that they were at the Galleria Academia museum to see the statue of David already, and that it would be about forty-five minutes before they got inside so we better get there quickly or they were going to go in without us. So much for my wistful thoughts of Dino. We hustled out of the Gardens and got to the museum in about forty-five minutes. No sign of Dino. I thought maybe he had decided the line was too long and had gone to find a statue of Randy instead. Finally, he texted us that the line had moved quicker than they had expected and they had seen the statue and gone back to the hotel. That was just as well, we could take our time in the museum now.

Even if you might have an idea of how magnificent the statue of David is, it still jumps out at you when you walk into the room. I liked watching all the older women trying to look very studious as they eyed David up and down ... until they got to his engine room. Then they would nod a little, smirk, and stare off into space for a second and resume walking. Carolyn would have stared off a little longer than the rest, but I pointed out that he had an even narrower waist than she did. That kept her moving pretty sprightly.

Eventually we caught up with Dino and Cathy outside our hotel and went to a little place to have a drink before dinner. It was the kind of place you see in the movies, with little tables outside and music coming from somewhere. Ten dollars for a beer, just like home—if you live in Yankee Stadium. It was nice ... one beer's worth of nice. While we had been seeing the Boboli Gardens and the *David*, Jackie was napping in our hotel room. The "bed" at her apartment was really just a metal frame with a two-inch pad on top. The only problem was she took her nap at our hotel during the only three hours a day that the construction guys happened to work without a twenty-minute break.

At dinner time we swung back by the hotel and picked up Jackie to join us. We walked around a little while and ended up eating at an outdoor restaurant near the Duomo called Trattoria al Corrallo. When we got home, I looked up the name. I couldn't find an exact translation, but I think it means "restaurant that tastes like a corral." We had had such good luck with little outside places in Rome that I thought this would be more of the same. Wrong. Carolyn didn't like the food at all. I blamed her. She had ordered veal Milanese, which is basically a breaded, fried veal cutlet with a lemon on top. I'm sorry, but that's Italian equivalent of an American cheese sandwich. Jackie had pasta with truffle sauce, and it was great. Dino didn't care for his dinner at all and was letting me have it. You see, this was all my fault because Carolyn had said, "How about this place?" and I didn't say no. I didn't write down what the others got for dinner because

I knew one night when we were having great food Dino would say, "Yo, Pete, get out your little notebook and tell me what I got that night you made us go to the place that sucked." Even Cathy, who never complains, couldn't come up with anything positive to say about it, and then she threw her plate at me. Well, that part's not true, but Cathy not being pleasant about things like that is the same as other people throwing a plate at you. It was a little bit nice that _my_ food was better than Dino's, but not very.

We walked around town for a little while after dinner but decided not to make it a late night. When I got back to the room I dived right into writing. There were some really funny ideas about how Jackie would get acclimated to the way things work here and how people get things done differently than at home. Maybe I would throw in some mystery man relationship to keep female readers interested. I decided to wait until I was done with the outline before showing it to Carolyn. This was going to be great. I couldn't believe how this idea had just sprung into my mind so completely.

The next day Vincenzo was coming back to take us to Cinque Terre, so I wrapped up the writing at about midnight and got some sleep.

September 18: According to Dino

I'm not sure why we feel compelled to go to the train station early to get the tickets to Venice, but we do. Just Peter and me. The girls stay in, or go out, or … whatever. It is a nice stretch of the legs that morning, and we have the freedom to ogle Italian women without worrying about being blatant about it. (In other words, swiveling our heads like Linda Blair in the Exorcist). And even better, we can openly comment on every one of them without fear of retribution from unreasonable and insecure spouses.

All Italian women look good—even the ugly ones. It is their sense of style, the way they walk, the way they talk, a certain flair. Like they all know they are Italian. Plus a lot of them have very perky hooters (a term Vincenzo evidently hadn't learned yet). Unfortunately, on the way to the station we have already bagged our legal limit of hot woman sightings, so we are forced to walk back talking about something other than attractive women. It wasn't easy. I had nothing except an idea I had for Pete's book. I tell him that he should make it a book of pictures of the babes on Vespas in Rome. He says he's not looking for a picture book. I tell him it would be a pop up book but he doesn't get it. Went about twenty feet right over his head. He doesn't say anything else for a while. I'm assuming that he's bummed about his lack of literary progress, but then I hear him mumbling about maybe we should, you know, split up for a while today, just them (the Grecos) and just us (Cathy and me), and then we can hook up later. Now, once again this has me very conflicted. On one hand, I can't believe my luck, but on the other hand, why is *he* bringing this up? What the hell is wrong with *us*? I can't figure it out, but I manage to keep my mouth shut and just nod my head, afraid that if I say something I may just blow this opportunity, which I clearly don't want to do.

When I get back to the room I tell Cathy about Pete's proposition, and she just looks at me and says, "OK." Not exactly the level of enthusiasm for our "alone" time that I am looking for.

What, in the name of everything holy, is going on here? I feel like I'm starting to lose control which is not good. Not good at all.

Pete and Carolyn tell us they intend to visit the Duomo this morning and are going to climb an incredible amount of steps to the platform on the top. I almost ask why, but I catch myself in time and say, "Sounds wonderful," instead. Cathy and I decide we just want to kick back today, so we leisurely meander through town, stopping at a few of the stores, just taking our time. This is one of the few times it's just the two of us, and we're both decompressing, not really saying much. You know when you're dating and there are periods of awkward silence? Well, after you get married they're not awkward anymore. In fact, if anything, the awkward times are when you actually have to talk to each other. Pete, despite being married, is the kind of guy who hates to have periods of what I consider blissful quiet, so he keeps up a steady stream of chatter at all times. I don't know how he does it. It's exhausting. I don't even know that many words. I notice that Carolyn pretty much monopolizes the conversations with Cathy as well. In her case, I think it's that after living with Pete for so long, she's just looking for an opportunity to get twenty years of pent up conversation out. Poor Cathy, but she actually doesn't seem to mind at all.

Anyway, now we're in this temporary work-release program from Greco State Prison, and I start subconsciously humming Simon and Garfunkel's *Sounds of Silence*. I can't get it out of my head. We walk slowly, enjoying the quiet. I pass a window and take a picture of an Italian dog (*cane*) lying there with one of those embarrassing plastic cones around his neck. He doesn't look happy, but he's an Italian dog, so who knows. Then, out of nowhere, Cathy starts talking about the Grecos: how nice they are, how much she likes the jacket they bought her, how much fun they are, blah, blah, blah. I'm telling you, the little hairs on the back of my neck are standing up. She isn't making any sense. Maybe the heat is getting to her. I steer her to the nearest trattoria and tell the guy, "My wife needs help. For the love of God, please seat us and get her something to drink." Cathy continues this incoherent babble. All I pick up are disjointed pieces, like, "Grecos," "Nice," "We should see them more often." Now I'm really getting worried. Finally the food and drink come, and she seems a little better. We get pizza made in brick ovens that cover an entire wall. Crust so thin you can see right through it. It is *perfetto*. We also got bruschetta. This is something we do a lot, because even though I'm not a huge bruschetta fan back home, the bruschetta (pronounced *broosh* KET *tah* not *brush* ET *tah* by the way) in Italy is delicious. First of all, the bread is great, they do this garlic something, something rub; virgin (how can they tell?) olive oil drizzle, then they layer on the best diced tomatoes you ever ate. It's unbelievable how something this simple can taste so damn good.

I have to admit that as much as I love to eat, I'm not a great cook. Pete is, but I'm not. Actually, Cathy isn't either. She mixes things OK, but if there's a need to apply heat, things have a tendency to go horribly wrong. But as I say, she's very hot. Even though I don't cook much, I do like watching the food channel. Not all of the chefs, just Giada De Laurentiis and Rachael Ray. And not all of their shows, either, just the ones where they show a lot of cleavage. It's funny, when they make great dishes—no cleavage. But when they make mac and cheese with pigs feet, they're half naked. I always look to see what they're making and Tivo all of the shitty-sounding meals. I don't think Cathy has caught on yet.

So we're having a real nice time, and it suddenly dawns on me. When it's just me and Pete, things are good. When it's just Cathy and me, everything's fine. It's only when Carolyn enters the picture that things go downhill in a hurry. Hmmmm.

After lunch we head over to the Galleria Academia to see the *David* statue. The line is long (Enzo told us this was the best time to get here and there wouldn't be any wait), but at least it moves quickly. The Grecos call Cathy's cell and tell us they're on their way, but we're already inside before they arrive, so they have to get in the back of the line. Inside, Cathy and I poke around a few outer rooms where we see examples of medieval art, then we enter a long hallway that has a small dome at the far end. Under the dome, standing majestically is the *David*. It's about twenty-five-feet tall and truly, truly amazing. It might simply have been how real it looked or maybe it was the intense expression on his face or maybe something else that I just can't explain but we're literally transfixed as we gaze at it. After a few minutes, I start looking at the faces of the other people milling around it. They have this look of awe and reverence as they stare at it, no one saying a thing. Cathy and I almost hadn't come, but we realized how glad we were that we didn't miss it. Of all the incredible things we saw in Italy, the *David* was the most memorable. I think the Grecos felt exactly the same way.

So speaking of the little devils, we're waiting for them when they finally meet us outside, and we decide to walk over to one of the piazzas in the center of Firenze. We grab an outdoor table just a few yards from an old-fashioned, beautifully ornate carousel that sits right in the middle of the square. Between us and the carousel is an Italian choir singing Beach Boys tunes. I wish. Actually, they sing some top twenty opera hits. Nothing you've ever heard of, but they sounded really good.

Sitting back, sipping a glass of nice Chianti, I'm really relaxed and looking forward to another wonderful dinner, but alas, that was not to be. You know why? Jackie. She threw off the whole chemistry of the four of us. Carolyn and Jackie were walking in front, and they stop at this *ristorante* just off the Duomo. All of the guidebooks say don't go to the restaurants right next to the major attractions, because they're usually tourist traps. Instead, go to the ones a little farther away. But Carolyn (See? Common denominator again) says, "How about this?" Now, normally I would say, "No fucking way," without even hesitating. But I see Jackie looking at her mother in that special way that a daughter looks up to her mom, and I don't have the heart to intrude on this truly screwed up moment. (I have boys). So we all sit down and eat the shittiest food we had in Italy. Everybody's complaining about the food, but no one is saying what everybody has to be thinking: this is Carolyn's fault. I vow that I'll never let sentiment overcome good judgment again, especially when there's food on the line.

For the rest of the night I am in a shitty mood, and unfortunately I take it out on my wife, which means I tell her that I want to have sex. Ordinarily, she would take this opportunity to let me know what a really bad idea that is in a way that only an Orien … , Asian woman can. But this time, she takes me by complete surprise and seems OK with the idea. So when we get back to the hotel I'm amazed that this is turning out to be a really great night. I'm even starting to throw a few new moves into the rotation when she suddenly blurts out, "Oh, Vincenzo!"

In the immortal words of Harry Chapin, "Another man might have been angry. Another man might have been hurt. But another man never would have …" Wanna know what I did? I'll tell you what I did. I did what any other self-respecting Italian would have done. I made believe I didn't hear it. What? What?

Friday, September 19: Peter's Version

Dino and Cathy had been talking up the trip to Cinque Terre almost since we started making plans. I didn't tell them I had never heard of the place until they mentioned it. When I did look it up, I still didn't get a clear concept of just what it was, so I was pretty curious when we left that morning. It was one of only two rainy days on the whole trip, but not that bad. It took a good couple of hours to get there. On the way, Vincenzo pointed out the mountains topped by Carrera marble. It looked like snow. I wondered how big those mountains were before they started taking all of that marble off the top. I didn't say anything out loud because I was sure there was some simple scientific explanation that everybody else knew that I didn't. ("Pete, what are you nuts? Marble grows back. You didn't know that? What a dope." And that would be Cathy talking.)

Cinque Terre (translated "five lands) is in northwest Italy, and is a series of five towns that are built into the hills dropping into the Mediterranean Sea. Because of the rugged terrain it is a little difficult to get to any of the five sections by car so many visitors, ourselves included, drive to the little seaside village of Portovenere to take a ferry to the first of the five lands, Riomaggiore. From there we planned to walk through all five villages and Vincenzo would drive directly to the end of the line to pick us up, unless he was called out to a stakeout or a treaty signing or something. As I said, it was raining a little when Vincenzo dropped us off. We bought our tickets for the ferry, but the next one wasn't due for about forty-five minutes, so we had coffee and a little nosh.

While we were waiting, a wedding was taking place in a nearby chapel. The bride and groom, both Asian, were walking through Portovenere in their wedding getups with people following them. Dino told us this is a tradition—not the Asian part, but the walking around part. He said the idea is that all the people in the town see you happy together one last time. The wedding party walked down the street all the way to the end of a dock. When there was no place left to go, they stopped and looked around. The groom seemed to be considering jumping into the marina and making a swim for it, but the bride had a death grip on his right hand, so they awkwardly smiled and returned to where they'd come from.

As they passed us, Dino waved to the groom, pointed to Cathy, and gestured as if to say, "I have also been fortunate to have an Asian wife." Then, when Cathy turned away, he pantomimed the gesture of hanging himself.

Right on schedule, the ferry came, and we were off. It was crowded, and we were packed into the back. The rain limited the number of dry places to sit. Since I was jammed in the middle of the crowded boat, Carolyn reluctantly agreed to take some pictures of the ferry ride. She normally doesn't like to take pictures, because she says everybody always criticizes her photography. All of her pictures look like she was jumping off a stool as she snapped them. Everything but the subject of the picture is in focus. She says it's not her fault, so I don't criticize her photography. I'm sure there must be something wrong with every camera we've ever owned.

As I said, Cinque Terre consists of five villages—Monterosso al Mare, Vernazza, Corniglia, Manarola, and Riomaggiore—built into the side of cliffs that drop right into the Mediterranean. The ferry doesn't stop at all of the towns and doesn't run that often so to get from one town to the other, you can walk a path that goes about seven miles, or you can take a train. The towns are actually very poor, depending on tourism and a little wine growing for most of their revenue. The vineyards are on very steep hills, and motorized contraptions can carry the grape pickers up and down so they don't fall to serious injury or death trying to maneuver themselves and the grapes. They *can* use the contraptions for this, but they don't. The motorized pulleys, baskets, and cables are used only for the grapes. ("Good luck, Vito. Sorry it's a little slick out there, but that basket of Vermentinos is worth a bundle; you I can replace with a dim-witted Calabrian.")

It was still raining, but the girls had brought umbrellas. I had bought a poncho, and Dino ordered the drops to stay the hell off him. It was a really nice walk in spite of the rain, with interesting terrain and dramatic views of the Mediterranean. The buildings were pastel colored and really beautiful against the hills. The walk was good, but getting a little harder. I think all four of us were thinking we'd really like a nice dry shuttle bus to take us the rest of the way. As we left Corniglia, the third of the five lands, the path was closed due to the wet weather. When I looked up Cinque Terre back home, I learned that the rest of the trip included a 380-step ascent, and some not-fun twists and turns. I would have had no problem, but Dino and the girls would have found that too taxing. Being adventurers, we thought quickly and called Vincenzo, begging him to come and get us. He told us to take the train from Corniglia to Vernazza, the next of the five lands. There he would meet us. The train (Trenitalia) cost about a dollar. We got on board with other wet tourists and locals who took the train to get home, or to pick pockets, or both.

It was a nice little train ride around and through the hills, lasting about eight minutes. We got off and found Vincenzo easily enough. From there he drove us through the hills to Monterosso al Mare, where we would have lunch; he said Vernazza wasn't all that great. On the way, we saw wild pigs rooting around. He suggested we not get out of the car to play with the pigs. I hadn't recalled hearing any of us say, "Ooh, wild pigs with big teeth, can we wrassle around with them?" But Carolyn and Cathy have very soft voices, so maybe I missed it. Monterosso al Mare was the nicest of the five lands and had a lot of shops and restaurants. We had a nice lunch in an outdoor café, which kind of annoyed me. Dino had conveniently forgotten Carolyn's role in choosing the restaurant the night before, so now we had eaten outside four times, and it had sucked only once—and I got nailed for it.

I need to point out here that Italy is the best country for cats. I am a dog person, always have been. There are pictures of me as a three-year-old wearing a Philadelphia Phillies hat and strangling a cat. I'm sure it was my brother's idea, but still, I was never a fan. As I got older, I built up more tolerance, but never really developed any affinity for them. But if all cats are like the ones in Italy, there might be some wiggle room.

Dino and Cathy have dozens of dogs and cats freely roaming their house, so they are already comfortable with large numbers of animals. Hell, Dino is a large number of animals. Now, we were eating outside in Cinque Terre, and right in the middle of the big outside patio area, sat a gray cat. People came up and took its picture, and it turned as if to pose for the photographer. It stayed there until everybody, including the four of us, took all the pictures they wanted. Then it got up to walk away, as if to say, "Next show at 2:30." But somebody else came up with a camera; the cat saw him, walked back to his spot, sat for a few more shots, then left. It turned out the cat's name was Bruno, and he worked for the restaurant and got room and board and tips. He replaced Ignatz, who'd had the job for seven years but got into catnip and a bad crowd of cats from behind the dumpster. Okay, so maybe my drunken idea in Rome about a lady meeting a dog who liked ice cream wouldn't work, but there is no reason I couldn't work in a cat to befriend Jackie in Florence. And this cat was excellent. Plus, we had that cat in Rome in the trellis at al Boschetta. Maybe the cat would be a composite, that's good, no worries about a cat libel suit.

After lunch we headed out of town. The roads were incredibly twisted, and more than a few times I had to resist the urge to scream, "We're gonna die!" At the top of a big hill we pulled over to the shoulder so everybody could take pictures from the highest point of the region—and I could kiss the pavement. I was shooting video of Cathy, Dino, and Carolyn looking over the vista with the road in the background. There was a sharp turn in the background. While I was filming, a car came around the turn and was heading right for the three of them. I didn't want to ruin the shot by putting the camera down to warn them, so I just calmly narrated the scene onto the video: "… and here is where the car came around the hill and killed my wife and our friends." But as the car approached, the road straightened out, and it wasn't even close. So now I had to figure out how to erase that clip and change my underwear before we got back to the hotel.

From Cinque Terre we went on to Lucca. We had inquired about going to Pisa, but Vincenzo advised against it. "You drive an hour, you look at the tower, and you get back in the car. Pisa is nothing. They got a tower in Lucca. Take a crooked picture, same thing." Lucca is the birthplace of Giacomo Puccini, the great composer of such operas as *Madame Butterfly*, *La Boheme*, *Tosca*, and *Turandot*. Dino commented that he didn't know Puccini composed all of those classic works, and that other than being answers in crossword puzzles, he wouldn't know *Tosca* from Bosco. We took a nice leisurely stroll through the town.

As was the case in every town or section of every city we would see in Italy, the shops were worth stopping for, even if just to see the displays. The Italians take their curb appeal very seriously. Sometimes there didn't even seem to be a connection between the window displays and their products; they just tried to catch your eye and entertain you. We passed one store in Lucca that had a mobile made out of different colored spoons hung from the ceiling. But you couldn't see the wire or string to which the spoons were attached. They appeared to be floating, suspended by magic. At first I thought it was an art gallery or maybe a store that sold kitchenware. But nope, it was a clothing store for young women. The freaking spoons weren't even for sale. I told Dino that was a cool idea; catch the wondering shopper's eye and seduce her into coming in to ask about the display. Dino disagreed, of course. He said that it was stupid not to have a bunch of the mobiles in stock to sell, and that if a woman went in and found out they couldn't buy the mobile they'd be pissed off and walk out. I then said something to the effect that Dino didn't know how women think. He looked at me incredulously and then looked at Cathy and Carolyn who would not make eye contact with him. "Is that true?" he said in their general direction. Cathy said, "Only in the sense that you don't care what women think, and you don't want to know what they think, honey." With that Dino paused for a second and said, "Oh, okay, well I can't disagree with you there, Pete."

Now Dino was paying more attention to the window displays as we wandered down more of the streets of Lucca. Finally we came to a window for a store that sold home decorations. On the floor there was a big tan dog with one of those inverted lamp shades around his neck that they use to prevent a dog from scratching himself after an operation. Dino took the dog's picture and said, "You know what, that dog sums up this vacation for me. He has that cone on his neck so now he can't lick his balls. That's one of the three or four things dogs really want to do, but he can't do it because they think he'll hurt himself. You guys are the cone around my neck. I can't do or say the things I really want to do because you guys won't let

139

me because it'll offend you or something." It was quiet for a few seconds and then I said, solemnly, "Dino, I know I speak for all of us when I say I'm sorry if we are inhibiting you. If you really want to lick your balls, you go right on ahead. We won't say a word." Dino looked me in the eye and said in all seriousness, "Thanks, Petey."

There was a square with a market in the middle of the town and we roamed through. At this point I could tell everybody's energy levels were lagging because Cathy and Carolyn were only half-heartedly regarding any of the merchandise and Dino walked past the only bar we saw without even slowing down to see if there was a St. Pauli girl poster inside. Vincenzo unenthusiastically offered to take us on a few more stops, sensing, maybe hoping that we had nothing left in the tank. He perked up dramatically when we told him we were done for the day, almost skipping to the car.

On the way back, Dino fell asleep. Just as he did, Vincenzo was merging onto a high-speed expressway at about seventy miles an hour. The traffic he was merging with was going about eighty-five and didn't make room for him. He suddenly began jutting in and out of traffic and swerving frantically between the road and the shoulder to avoid a crash that would have killed us all. If we weren't so tired, we would have screamed - which would have made everything all better, of course. The whole time he was doing this scene from *French Connection*, Vincenzo was cursing at every car he almost hit. The final jerking motion that got us back on the road woke Dino, who turned to us with his eyes half out of his head like he was glad he didn't know exactly what happened. I said to Vincenzo, "I guess you got a lot of training in high-speed driving so you can handle a car like that. " He replied very matter of factly, "No, I get no training. I did not see that guy coming. We almost got killed." We just kind of nodded, as if we had been informed that dying was an option with our tour and we had chosen the "near-death-experience-with-safe–return" package instead. I'm proud to say all four us escaped with our lives and our underwear intact, assuming Dino was wearing any to begin with.

Now refreshed from his power nap and brush with death, Dino started speaking in Italian. Thinking I couldn't understand him, he told Vincenzo I didn't have a father, just two mothers. I know more

Italian than I let on, and I told Dino my mother was not a lesbian. Then he went back to sleep, happy.

Vincenzo had a final restaurant recommendation for us, and he made a reservation while driving through Florence back to the hotel. We spent two full days with Vincenzo and felt we had developed a bond with him. Even if he had a 1952 view of women and almost killed us with his car, we developed a bond. So when Vincenzo dropped us off, we all got out of the car and went over to say good-bye to him one at a time. The girls hugged him and thanked him. Dino and I heartily shook his hand. And all the time the look on his face said, "What's wrong with these people? Why are they hugging me? I almost killed them. Just give me the money and let me take a quick nap before I dress up like a whore and try to catch heroin dealers." (Turned out he *was* an undercover narcotics cop). So with that, Vincenzo took our very generous tip from Dino and sped off, never to be seen or heard from again—unless we go back to Florence before he nods off and drives off a cliff.

With the workers done for the day, we were able to take a little nap. I only needed about fifteen minutes and woke up recharged. While Carolyn slept and even while she started getting ready I was plowing away at my outline. I decided I would have Jackie meet a new guy at the end instead of getting back with her old boyfriend so now I just needed to tie up a few loose ends before showing it to Carolyn. Carolyn was still deciding from among six outfits for dinner so I went out to the lobby with Dino. A few minutes later Cathy was ready and joined us. I tried to distract Dino with conversation about the restaurant Vincenzo recommended, Quattro Leone. Dino wanted nothing to do with it. He started pacing wordlessly, then, he looked at me and nodded toward our room and bugged his eyes out so emphatically I thought they would fly out of his head. I told him Where's Carolyn was just about ready when I left the room and was probably just putting on the finishing touches. Actually, I found out later that she was standing by the door waiting to hear Dino ask where the hell she was and eventually got tired of waiting and joined us in the lobby. I told her she looked lovely and it was worth the wait. Dino muttered something about asking Enzo for the name of a good assassin.

Quattro Leone was across the Ponte Vecchio and down a side street. It had indoor and outdoor seating, and we got a nice table outside. As I have said too often by now, the food in Italy was even better than I had anticipated. This night we had excellent wine, and I admit I was extremely relaxed and happy by the time dinner arrived. I had taglierini al tartufo nero de stagione, which I roughly translate to an orgasm with black truffle cream sauce and shaved truffles on top. When it arrived I took a bite and involuntarily pounded the table with my fist, yelling, "Oh my God!" It was as if I had found five thousand dollars in my pants pocket, assuming five thousand dollars could buy me a lifetime supply of this stuff. I tried to eat slowly, but it was impossible. I shared with everybody, but reluctantly. I told Carolyn she could have the next couple of days off from marital responsibilities. She said, "OK, thanks for the notice, but since when is that your call, pal?" I didn't care. The rest of the night is a blur. I might have proposed to the waiter, I'm not sure. I think we saw Jackie and some of her friends near il Duomo and got some gelato. If I did any writing I never found any sign of it the next morning. Years from now I will tell people, "Yeah, I was in Italy. I saw the Colosseum, the Vatican, the Forum (I think), the Pantheon, Michelangelo's *David*, *The Birth of Venus*, and all that other stuff, blah, blah, blah, but let me tell you about this spaghetti ...

Friday, September 19: According to Dino

This morning we're all supposed to meet Vincenzo again. Cathy's looking at me a little sheepishly. Maybe it was all the lamb chops she ate the night before, but personally I think it's because of the little Vincenzo incident the night before. I don't say anything, but I'm half tempted to tell her, "Guess what, Missy? I was this close to yelling, 'Mario!' last night." No. I'm kidding. That would be sick. I'd never do that. Seriously.

We get up early, meet my wife's version of an Italian blowup doll, and head out to Cinque Terre. Cinque Terre, which means five lands, are five picturesque villages carved out of the mountains overlooking the Mediterranean Sea. Today they're connected via a narrow, winding, man-made trail carved through the sides of the mountains, and also a railroad line, but in the old days people couldn't get from one town to the other. I suspect that one of the townspeople, probably the one with three ears and six toes (he was the only one with three ears; they all had six toes), decided it would be a lot better for the gene pool if they found an easy way to travel between the towns, so they started building the trail. Try to find that little tidbit on the Discovery Channel.

On the way to Cinque Terre, as we drive through more of Tuscany, we are treated to an incredibly beautiful landscape along the way. Cathy points to a little village situated around the top of a hill. Vincenzo tells her it's a centuries-old monastery. Pete sees a large mountaintop that's being quarried and asks if we can get a good price on Carrera marble if we polish it ourselves. Vincenzo says that by the looks of Pete and me, we probably polish a lot of things by ourselves. I hear a female giggle from the back seat, and I swear it's not Carolyn. I'm starting to think about ways I can polish off Vincenzo.

By the time we get to Portovenere, where we catch the ferry to the first of the towns of Cinque Terre, it's starting to rain. This is the first bad weather we've had so far. There's a small café there, so we all decide to grab a cup of cappuccino and wait it out. Vincenzo says he'll take the car and meet us when the ferry lands. He may be after my wife, but I gotta admit, he's a damn good guide.

It's still drizzling when the ferry picks us up, and it's only a short ride before we arrive at the first town, Riomaggiore. You walk right through the middle of the town to pick up the trail to the next town, which gives us an excellent opportunity to view all the laundry hanging from almost every window we pass. I do my best to look in some of the windows, but the only thing I see is an old lady taking a sponge bath. I will never, never, never, never, never do that again. It's still drizzling as we start down the connecting trail, and Pete and I are still leading, but now we're so far ahead of the girls that we can't see them anymore. We start to think that they were possibly abducted by some six-toed Riomaggiorians to use as fresh breeding stock. Now there's a hell of a story idea for Pete's book. The girls get abducted and Pete and I try to rescue them but we get side tracked by a couple incredible looking Italian babes and we party with them for days, forgetting all about the wives until we get on the plane home and … Yeah, that's some good material. Pete's going to love it.

Still no sign of the girls and we are becoming mildly concerned, but then we see them turn the corner. Boy, are we slightly relieved. It takes about twenty minutes until we get to the next town, Manarola. It's pretty much the same, but the laundry looks dirtier. Then Corniglia. More of the same, but no laundry. Wonder what that means? We continue on our way but have to stop because they close the trail. Someone says there's a landslide ahead, but I realize that it is, after all, an Italian trail and it probably just went on strike. Either way, we're screwed. Cathy calls Vincenzo and tells him what happened, and he tells her that we should take the train to Vernazza, where he'll pick us up. I don't hear any hint of anything going on between them until the end, when I hear her say, "No, you hang up. No, you hang up." I'm starting to get partially pissed.

Pete tells us we should get on the train, but I'm afraid we're going to end up in Sicily. I ask a few people, and they say in

Italian, "Yes, indeed, he does look very stupid, but in this case, somehow, your friend managed to get it right." I'm skeptical, but sure enough, a few minutes later, we're in Vernazza. When we get off the train, I see a poster that's hanging on a wall in the train station and take a picture. It was done so well and the detail was so lifelike, that even my photo looks like real fruit. Even the posters are works of art. Soon we see Vincenzo walking toward us, and we're all glad to see him, especially my wife, who runs up to him and jumps into his arms, which, to this day, I still believe was inappropriate. He has to drive up a steep mountain road to get to another road that will take us to Monterosso al Mare. In English that means, uh, Monterosso of the Sea. I ask Vincenzo if there's a city called Pollo al Mare, which would mean Chicken of the Sea. Guess they don't have canned tuna here because he just looks at me wondering what the hell I'm talking about.

Anyway, Vincenzo stops the car at a pull-off near the top, on the edge of the mountain. The grapevines are growing all along this almost-ninety-degree incline, and I ask how the people get up and down the sides of the mountain to pick them. Vincenzo says, "Very carefully." I'm trying to see how it can be done, leaning over the abyss, when I feel someone push against me from behind. Unbelievably, I don't go over, and I'm able to quickly turn around, expecting to see Vincenzo. But he was nowhere in sight. Only Cathy was there, mumbling, "Be careful, honey." Weird isn't it?

We then hear the grunts of a pack of wild boars moving through the trees on the safe side of the street. Now, I know that pigs can dispose of a human body in no time (Discovery Channel), and I'm thinking that a few of these babies could probably go through Vincenzo faster than my cousin Alfonse could knock off a plate of veal saltimbocca. Something to keep in mind. Yes sir, something to ... keep ... in ... mind.

When we get to Monterosso, we find a nice little place to eat that overlooks a small marina. The rowboats are all painted different colors, and they gently rock back and forth as you sit back and sip your vino. I seriously don't remember being this relaxed without the aid of pharmaceutical assistance and I'm getting tired of saying this but once again, the food is wonderful. Carolyn gets spaghetti with black ink squid sauce. Sounds gross, right? But I have a taste, and it is fantastic. These Italians are amazing. They could make snails taste good. Well, actually, that's escargot, so maybe not the best analogy, but you get the picture.

A *gato* (cat) is sitting by one of the tables, and everybody is taking pictures of him. I really don't get what the big attraction is, but I suddenly realize what this cat needs: an agent. I'm this close to putting out an empty hat and a sign that says, "Out of Work. I won't use Euros to buy catnip." This could be better than the fake flute scam, and I'm sure I can talk the cat into giving me 10 percent. But I remember now that I have to keep an eye on Cathy (which frees up Pete), and realize that I just don't have the energy to save my marriage *and* take advantage of this opportunity to make a few extra bucks. This is a real dilemma, until finally the cat walks off, which makes my decision much easier. I'm saving my marriage, damn it!

On the way out of town, Vincenzo pulls over again so we can take some pictures. Yeah, right. I stay in the van. When everyone gets back in, we decide to head over to a town called Lucca. We have never heard of it before, but I like the sound of it because Luca Brasi is my all-time favorite literary character. You know, the guy who sleeps with the fishes from *The Godfather*. I cry every time I watch Sonny get the flounder wrapped in newspapers. I can see the look on his face as he unwraps it and says, "What the hell is this?" Talk about a poignant scene. I'm getting choked up just thinking about it now.

Lucca isn't far, and there is something about this town that I fall in love with. It has a big dirt-and-stone wall that goes all around the city and was used as a defense during medieval times, but today it's a place where people jog and ride their bikes on Sunday afternoons. This is Italy so, obviously, there's a major square in the city, and I know this sounds crazy, but it has the feel of a quaint New England town. We meander around the streets looking into the shops and buying a few things from carts set up along the walks. I really want to come back here someday and spend more time just hanging out and getting to know the people. I wanted to stay longer and soak up more of this great atmosphere, but everyone else is getting tired, so we get back on the road. Vincenzo asks us if we want to go to another town on the way back, but we're bushed and we tell him we'll call it a day.

A few miles from Lucca, Vincenzo merges onto the highway that will take us back to Florence. Actually, merge isn't a good description, as it implies that he would work his way into the traffic. In this case, it looks like he is actually trying his best to simultaneously broadside a truck, two cars, and at least one motorcycle. As he attempts this feat, I hear everyone in the back seat simultaneously inhale, which makes me light-headed from the sudden lack of oxygen. Just before this I briefly had my eyes closed as I was hoping to take a quick nap, but I saw the whole thing. After we miraculously make it onto the highway unscathed, I say:

Dino: "Hey Vincenzo, do me a favor."

Vincenzo: "Sure, what favor?"

Dino: "Next time you do something like that, make sure you wake me up first."

Vincenzo: "Why?"

Dino: "Because I've never seen a big accident before."

He just frowns and sneaks a little grin into the rearview mirror. I doubt that he's looking at Pete. I can hear Carolyn snoring, so I'm thinking there's definitely something going on between him and my wife. Unfortunately, I'm outta eyes.

I think his driving on the highway is bad, but it is even worse when we get back to Florence. He's whipping around things like a maniac, and he finally tells me that he knows where all the traffic cameras are located, and he doesn't want someone in the Carabinieri to see him and four American tourists cruising through Florence in his car, because moonlighting as a tour guide is frowned upon. I see him shoot another lustful look into the rearview mirror. It's like he's saying he's good at doing things and not getting caught. Go ahead, I'm thinking, go for it. She leaves me for you, and five minutes later I'm on the phone with a certain hotel clerk in Rome.

When Vincenzo drops us off, we pay him, and then while walking toward the hotel, I hear Cathy say, "Oh, wait, I forgot to give him a tip." She's trying to pull the wool over my eyes. (Once again she should really cut back on the lamb chops). But I didn't just fall off the mozzarella truck, so I say, "You head back to the hotel, honey. I'll bring him the tip." She looks a little dejected, but what can she do? You gotta get up pretty early to get one over on me, baby. Actually, she did get up pretty early that day, but it still didn't work. I walk off, grab an espresso and a shot of sambuca, pocket the tip, and tell everybody how grateful he was. Back on my game.

It's getting late, so we agree that nap time is out but we will freshen up and meet in twenty minutes. Cathy, Pete, and I are waiting in the hallway twenty minutes later. I repeat: Cathy, Pete, and I are waiting in the hallway. I say, for the one hundred and thirty-fourth time over the last ten days, "Where's Carolyn?" I've been saying this so often that after a while I just start calling her that, like it's her full name. I say, "Hey, where's Carolyn, how are you feeling?" Or, "Good morning, where's Carolyn, how did you sleep last night?" You'd think she'd get the point.

Finally she comes out of her room, and her hair is all frizzed out like an Afro. But it's brown, sort of, and she's this pale Irish chick, so it's really pretty scary. After that, we call her "Where's Sophia," figuring she now looks more like a curly haired Italian babe. We head over to the restaurant Quattro Leone, or Four …

Leone. Cathy and I are walking behind the Grecos, and from behind it looks like Pete is holding hands with Germaine Jackson. Fookin hilarious. Anyway, once again, the food is out of this world. Me, Pete, and Where's Sophia are drinking vino di casa like crazy. Cathy's drinking sparkling water, which can be called either *frizzante* or *con gas*. Since *con gas* doesn't sound too appetizing, we usually ask for *aqua frizzante*. Later, as we are scouring downtown for a new gelato shop, we see Jackie and some of her friends, more American students who are also there wasting their parents' money. We hit the bed just about the time Jackie and her friends are heading out to the clubs. I'm sure they'll study later.

Saturday, September 20: Peter's Version

Today was our last full day in Florence, my new favorite city in the world. I was starting to get a cold; maybe that would be the price of a great vacation. The four of us had some breakfast and decided to split up for a while. Dino and Cathy wanted to do some shopping, and Carolyn and I wanted to go to the Basilica di Santa Croce. The four of us arranged to meet at the basilica so we could walk over the Ponte Vecchio again and just enjoy the city one more time. The basilica is the burial place of people like Dante, Galileo, Michelangelo, Marconi—it's a veritable dead guy hall of fame. I think Sinatra made a play to get in there, but he ended up in Southern California. We hadn't really done too much cathedral visiting on the trip so far. I could only think of two or three we went to as a group. I had gone to another three or four with Carolyn or by myself, you know, trying to atone for having a good time.

The basilica was very interesting. The façade was designed by a Jewish architect. He didn't get to be buried inside though. They buried him under the porch, literally. This place was definitely more tourist stop than religious facility—you don't often pay to get into a church—but the artwork of the tombs was impressive. Attached to the back of the basilica was what used to be a Franciscan dormitory and is now the Scuola del Cuoio, or School of Leather. This got Dino very interested, but it turned out to be a school that teaches leather-making—the socially acceptable kind. Carolyn and I went through the basilica and then walked around back, where we found the school. As we approached the entrance, we looked across a lot and saw a small garage or storage shed with a metal roof. Lying on the roof was a cat. It was a cat on a hot tin roof. Get it? Yeah, not as funny when you retell it, I guess. Maybe it would have been better if we'd bought that glass menagerie we saw in Rome.

Anyway, the school of leather was interesting. You could watch bored leather workers make wallets. In Asia this is called a sweatshop; in the U.S. it would be considered occupational therapy. Actually, the workmanship was excellent, and all of it for sale, but once you got beyond a change purse or a bookmark, the prices were a little nuts. Carolyn wanted to buy me a wallet, but none of them had pictures of present or former Philadelphia Phillies etched into them, so I opted for a leather toothpick. Not really effective.

When we were finished with the school, Carolyn and I soaked up some sun in front of the basilica. Dino and Cathy came by, and we gave them our tickets to the basilica. I don't carry a stopwatch, but I think they got through the basilica in about fifty-seven seconds. We strolled through the leather goods in the school with them and were back out on the street. Since this was our last day in Florence, we thought it best to just relax and walk around town. We'd already decided not to take any chances on dinner that night. We would return to Marione, where we went on our first night in Florence. Casually strolling around, Dino and I were already making plans for a return trip. I mentioned that Carolyn and I were thinking of going to Ireland as well. He said that was fine, and maybe we could take Cathy with us; he would just wait for us in Italy.

Every day we noticed people drawing on the streets with chalk, making fabulous portraits for tips. I'm not sure what kind of money they made doing this; they didn't make anything off me, although I think Carolyn slipped one of the guys a few Euros when he indicated he was using her as his model for the chin for his drawing of Venus. Dino walked by these guys and commented on how good the drawings were, and how they probably drew the same thing every day twice a day, so no wonder they were pretty good. No tip from Dino.

There were a few more expeditions into shops and outdoor markets, but I don't think Carolyn and I bought anything else. We were going to go back to our rooms a little early so we could start packing and not be rushed the next morning, and I was already thinking we wouldn't be able to fit everything we'd bought into our bags: olive oil, pasta, ties, change purses, and Carolyn's boots, handbag, and pashmina. Now I was thinking, holy cow, Dino and Cathy … Cathy bought a ton of stuff while we were walking, and we had given her that coat. As we were discussing what we had to pack, Cathy got quiet and started looking in store windows. They had to be approaching the breaking point for their bags. Maybe they would need to ship some stuff home. Dino said they could probably fit what they'd bought so far, so they would be OK if Cathy didn't buy anything in Venice. Cathy looked at Dino. Dino looked at Cathy. Dino looked at me and asked how much I thought it would cost to send either what they had bought or Cathy back to the states in a FedEx box. Cathy asked if we could stop by one store for a minute. She went in, and Carolyn, Dino, and I waited outside. Then Dino looked in after Cathy. She was looking at luggage. "Son of a bitch!" Dino said. "She's buying luggage to pack the stuff she bought!" She got a very attractive cloth bag that could hold almost everything they'd bought so far. I'm sure they'll get a lot of use out of it in the years to come. Carolyn was very supportive of Cathy, because as long as Cathy had more stuff, there was a little more she could get.

We saw Jackie one last time so Carolyn could enjoy a nice cry, then went to dinner. Marione didn't disappoint. I know we probably should have tried another place, but it just seemed unlikely we would find anything much better, and the risk was simply too big. That night we enjoyed one more walk around town, then turned in early.

While Carolyn tried to get everything she had accumulated on the trip thus far, I finished up the outline. Just as she finished packing, I handed her the pages and asked her to give me her honest opinion. My wife is incapable of lying. She is totally capable of withholding large portions of the truth, but she is incapable of lying. Plus she is a tough audience. When I work on stand-up bits I run them past her. If I get so much as a half smile I know the material is worth keeping, so I was carefully watching her expression as she slowly read the material. Also, being trained as a paralegal Carolyn reads painfully slowly often pointing out tiny grammatical errors as she goes; very annoying when you just want the big picture.

As she read, a confused look came over her face. She stopped a couple of times and looked off as if trying to remember something. She finished and put the papers down.

Peter: Well?

Carolyn (hesitantly): It's good. It's funny…

Peter: But what…you aren't too enthusiastic

Carolyn: ...I think it's better than the movie, but not as good as the book.

Peter: What do you mean the movie?

Carolyn: You basically rewrote the screenplay for *Under the Tuscan Sun*.

Peter: Huh?

Carolyn: Remember that movie, *Under the Tuscan Sun*? I really liked the book. You didn't read it. Then we rented the movie. Not as good as the book

Peter: Huh?

Carolyn: I remember you lost interest in the movie and started working on a Sudoku. Then you got frustrated with that and set fire to it and threw it in the fireplace.

Peter: That one was hard. It was three stars out of five...Oh my God! I rewrote *Under the Tuscan Sun?*! I didn't even watch the bloody thing. How could I absorb that much when I was sleeping...but you say it's funny?

Carolyn: Yeah, if they decided to make that movie a comedy, this would have really helped. But it's almost the same freaking thing.

Peter: Oh my God, I have nothing to show this guy on Tuesday. What the hell!

Carolyn: (Thinking back) That's the day I bought that boat neck sweater and those really comfortable black shoes... remember? What happened to those shoes? I really wanted to bring them with us. I hate when I can't find things...

Peter and Carolyn: Damn it!

Needless to say I didn't get much sleep. It was a once in a lifetime opportunity to have a book idea read by a legitimate literary agent and I blew it. Why had I been so careless? How could I have taken my eye off the ball? How much of this could I blame on Dino?

September 20: According to Dino

I'm the first one up, so I hit the bathroom and take a shower. A few minutes later, I come back looking for my other pair of underwear. As I look over to see if Cathy's awake yet, I can't believe my eyes. There's my wife, playing hide the mortadella with someone right in my hotel room, right under my nose! The guy is under the covers, and I grab the sheets as fast as I can and rip them off expecting to see you know who. I start to yell, and to my amazement it's not Vincenzo. It's Mario! But he's got this brown, sort of, Afro. Like a big rusty Brillo pad. Exactly like Carolyn's. And they're both laughing at me!

That fucking Bolognese sauce! This is a dream. So I'm standing there, and you know when you're dreaming and sometimes you know that it's a dream? Well, that's what happens to me. So I jump into bed between my wife and Mario. No, I'm kidding. I just wake up. Really. Seriously, I would never do that. That's sick. In fact, I hardly ever even think about Mario anymore.

OK, so it's Sunday morning, and I realize it's just a dream, and I'm really upset now, because in my dream I had already shaved and taken a shower, and now I realize that I have to do them all over again. But first I shake Cathy and start yelling, "Do you know what time it is? We have to get to church!!" No matter what I do, I can't get her to wake up. Sorry, God.

This is the last day in Firenze. To be honest, Florence has been great, and definitely different than Rome (which I still like the best), and driving through Tuscany with all of the side trips was something I'll never forget but I'm really ready to move on and see Venice. Today the four of us decide that we'll all do our own thing again. Cathy wants to do some shopping, and let's face it, Carolyn would only slow her down. So we walk around town, but now we're spending a lot more time in many of the shops that Cathy pretended she wasn't interested in when she was with Carolyn.

I stay outside taking pictures and Pete finally texts us that they hit the Basilica di Santa Croce and have free tickets if we want to come over and use them. Frankly, I think he was just getting tired of the throngs of tourists coming up to Carolyn asking if she minded if they take a photo of them standing next to her hair but what the hell. Anything that gets Cathy to stop spending money is fine with me. We get to the basilica pretty quickly, grab the freebee tickets, and the wife and I go in. All along the walls are a series of extremely ornate burial chambers of some of the most important Italians this side of the Rat Pack. Michelangelo, Dante, and Galileo are all buried there.

In a courtyard behind the basilica is the Scuola del Cuoio (School of Leather). There are a lot of leather stores in this area, but this is where the artisans are trained. They have a small store there, too, so we go in and buy a few things. I ask them where the whips are, but no one finds that as funny as I thought they would. Instead we pick up a few leather bookmarks (something you can never have too many of) and a wallet for my dad.

This is supposed to be a pretty laid-back day, one where we don't have to be anywhere in particular or plan things around a schedule, so on the one hand it's really enjoyable, on the other hand, a little boring. But then again, this is Florence, freaking, Italy, so what the hell? We are taking our time as we lazily stroll through the quiet streets. It's Sunday, and not much is happening, but we don't mind at all. We're ready to make a pit stop for a few Peronis and some happy-hour complimentary salami and cheese at an Osteria, but I see a bookstore across the street, and when I walk over, I see that in the window is an English version of a Ray Bradbury book, *The Martian Chronicles*. I actually laugh out loud because this is the focus of a somewhat sore subject between me and the little lotus blossom.

For years my wife has been harassing me about how evil I am and how wacky my family is. She says "D'Adamo" as if it's Italian for "Lucifer," which brings me to the book. In *The Martian Chronicles*, a family goes to Mars to help colonize it. When they get there, all they see are ruins of an ancient Martian civilization, but there are no Martians left. After a few years, the father announces to the family that they're all going to see real Martians that day. Everybody's excited, and they go off trudging through the ruins, and after hours of walking, they find a little boat. They row out to the middle of a big Martian lake, and the kids are yelling, "When are we going to see the Martians, Daddy?" He says, "Look down." They all do, and they see their own reflections in the water. The father says, "There's the Martians." So anyway, every once in a while, when my wife goes off on one of her D'Adamo tirades, I pull her in front of a mirror and I say, "But honey, look, *we're* the D'Adamos." She then lets out a bloodcurdling scream. Seriously. Every time. Once, she actually cracked the mirror.

I really enjoy doing that, and I'm still smiling when I rejoin the others, who are now seated outside, snacking and sipping Italian beer. Cathy has ordered me a glass of cold Peroni and it's waiting patiently as I take my seat. The foamy head clinging to the top of my beer glass is enticing me as few women ever have been able. I quickly chug the golden nectar and while sighing (and burping), I find myself peering down a long cobblestone street as the sun starts to fade, and I realize that the Italians have it right: life is sweet, but how seldom we stop for an *assagiare* (taste). *La vita e troppo breve,* (Life is just too damn short).

That night, we're once again the first in line at Marione. I'm now acutely aware of the potential dangers of disturbing dreams brought on by tortellini Bolognese, so you can imagine my surprise when I open my mouth to order and those exact words come tumbling out. I can't help it. It's such a fantastic dish. As I eat, I realize there's a good chance I'll never be back there, and a single tear rolls down my now bulging cheek. When we're done, the waitress comes by and I ask her if they have canoli. She looks right at me, sticks her finger in the air, and says, "No!" No hesitation, no apologetic tone. Just, "No!" It takes me by surprise, so I do the same thing to her and say, "No?" while sticking my finger in the air and using the same clipped Italian accent. Even she finds that funny, but it doesn't change the fact that they don't have canoli. Hey, at least she understood what the hell I was asking for. I feel slightly vindicated, but no less hungry for dessert, so after dinner we do the obligatory gelato shuffle. This is what all Italians do. They don't wolf (*lupo*) down an early meal and then sit on their fat asses watching TV. They eat dinner late, take their time, walk, socialize, have sex, then sit on their fat asses and watch TV.

We turn in, and I try to finish the rest of the grappa in our room, because we don't want to pack it. I'm doing a pretty good job on it but am feeling amazingly sober, considering the amount of alcohol I've managed to consume. Maybe I'm building up a tolerance. I hope not. Tomorrow (*domani*), Venice!

View from the top of the Duomo in Florence. You can see the people who went to the top of the Campanile next door. We yelled over that we climbed higher than they did. They yelled back that they took an elevator and stopped halfway up for gelato.

Here is the center of Siena where they run the Pallia. The people sitting down are part of a tour group from Seaside Heights, New Jersey. One of them smelled suntan lotion and they all sat down and waited for the tide to come in

On the streets of Florence: Sidewalk artists are found throughout the city. Dino would walk by, look at the drawing for a minute, and then tell them they got the mouth wrong.

Dead Couple Walking. An Asian bride and groom taking the traditional walk in Portovenere. Notice how everybody is looking away. That's because what you can't tell from the picture is that the groom is sobbing hysterically.

This cat, we called him "Bruno" worked the room at an outside café in Monterosso al Mare in Cinque Terra. He would leave to enthusiastic applause and go back to his dressing room behind the dumpster

Seriously, a cat on a hot tin roof outside of El Scuolo de Cuoio (School of Leather) in Florence. There was a pack of dogs doing Streetcar in the parking lot.

Part 4:   Venice: The Gondolier's Going Down

Sunday, September 21: Peter's Version

It was Sunday and early, so I thought I'd better walk over to one of the churches on the off chance a mass was starting just so I could beg for a miracle. But my epic timing held, and none of the five churches I passed had a mass scheduled within the next half hour, so I ended up going in and just praying by myself. Just the basics: thanks for the nice trip, please take care of my kids, and what the hell do I do about having zip to show this bloody literary agent. I know it's not God's problem. He already gave us a nicer vacation than I had any right to expect. Lastly I asked that whatever else was going to go wrong to balance out how much fun we've had, please make it as quick and painless as possible.

In addition to the revelation that I was a subconscious plagiarist, it was cloudy, the end of the trip was near, and when I came back to the hotel I discovered Dino hadn't decided to fly home early, so I was a little down when the day started. We were heading north and east to Venice. Many of the friends I had spoken to before we left told me Venice was the most beautiful of the three cities. Still I must have had a miserable expression on my face because even Dino noticed. For Dino to sense some that somebody else is unhappy they would normally have to have one end of a rope around their neck and the other tied to a load-bearing ceiling beam. He said nothing all the way to the train station.

Our train was scheduled to leave at 11:40 a.m. We got to the station in plenty of time and had no problem finding the right platform. We had seats 16, 24, 47, and 9, all right next to each other again. This time we sat with our spouses. I think we were feeling romantic—Italy was having an effect. The train would stop in Bologna, Rovigo, and Padua. While waiting for the train to pull out, I read up on the layout of Venice, and experienced a little more anxiety. The guidebook said it was harder to find your way in Venice than other Italian cities, and there was a bigger risk of petty theft and pick pocketing. What was more, the forecast was for rain, and

165

we weren't going to be in the same hotel because Dino and Cathy were using airline points to get an upgraded place. Carolyn and I picked a place online. For a control freak like me, this was a perfect storm.

We sat down and as the train pulled out Dino looked over at me and said, "Pete, what the fuck is bothering you? We're in Italy. We're going to Venice. It's been a great trip for you, even at the expense of me enjoying myself. How can you be bummed out?" Since any hope of the book happening was lost and I was feeling so miserable I told him. "I got nothing! The damn book. I'm out of time. On Tuesday I'm meeting the literary agent, or at least I was. He was going to look over the outline and maybe set it up for me to get the book published. But last night I finished the outline and Carolyn read it and realized I had basically rewritten a screenplay." Dino was incredulous. "What screenplay?" I told him, "*Under the Tuscan Sun*" At that even Cathy laughed, "Peter," she said, you rewrote *Under the Tuscan Sun* and didn't realize it? I mean, loved the book but the movie, not so much. Why didn't you re-write the book instead?" At that all three of us looked at Cathy until she said, "Oh…right." Then Dino blurted out, "What about the pop up book? No? I got another idea. You're going to love it." I only *think* Dino kept talking because I could see his lips moving but didn't hear another word he said. When he was done, we were quiet for about ten minutes until Dino mumbled, "What the hell made you think you could write a fucking book?"

For some reason, that comment struck me funny, almost as though Dino had said it about somebody else. So I thought, what the hell, toughen up. Why make things worse, let's make the best of this mess. As painful and embarrassing as it was I decided the thing to do was simply turn the page (how can I think of puns at a time like this) and try to enjoy the rest of the trip. The next two hours of the train ride were spent thinking of how to explain my goose egg to the publisher and how to avoid falling/jumping into the Grand Canal.

We arrived in Venice right on time. Just as advertised, there were plenty of water taxis to take us to our hotels. Dino explained to the pilot where our hotels were, but we got there fine anyway. He told the pilot to drop Ernest and Connie Hemingway off first.

Venice is interesting geographically. It is an island split into six districts separated by canals, with bridges of various sizes connecting the sections. Dino and Cathy were staying in San Marco, the upscale district most people think of when they picture Venice. We were staying in a section just to the west of San Marco called Dorsoduro. Dorsoduro is the more bohemian district of Venice, a little less classy and artsy, but less expensive. In other words the poor side of town.

We were staying at the Hotel Diphtheria on Ca'Rezzonico which is a canal on Vaporetto line 1. The vaporetti are small motorboats which move on specified routes throughout Venice. The vaporetti cruise a route much like a taxi and pick up and drop off passengers along the route. Our hotel was about a two-hundred-yard walk from where the vaporetto dropped us off, and we walked along a narrow sidewalk with buildings on our left and a canal on our right. The hotel building was nondescript—a nice way of saying unattractive. Once inside, it wasn't a lot better, but it seemed safe and clean. The man behind the desk didn't seem too excited to see us. Even I was getting a little misty-eyed for Mario at this point. This clerk made us cool our heels in the lobby for a few minutes and then unenthusiastically led us upstairs to the second floor and our room. Did you ever hear the expression "a little hole in the wall" to describe someplace? Well, this was that place. Plus, when we opened the curtains, there was a hole in the wall.

At the beginning of this journal, I mentioned the room we had on our cruise with Dino and Cathy. The bathroom in this hotel made the one on the cruise seem like the grotto at the Playboy Mansion. Carolyn was a little dejected. She had found the place, and we both liked it online, so there was nobody to blame. That was a little disappointing, but what are you going to do? We wouldn't spend much time in the room; in fact we couldn't, considering that one of us had to leave the room if the other one wanted to get dressed or turn around. But there was a Grom for gelato at the end of the block, and we were saving a lot of money, and there would be fewer pickpockets since nobody staying here had any money. Plus there was a nice breakfast room, and, as we learned later, the breakfast attendant was friendlier than anybody else on the staff.

Dino and Cathy stayed at the Westin Europa in San Marco. After the weather cleared up a little, Carolyn and I were able to find the Europa and met them on the sidewalk outside. We decided to check out St. Mark's Square. This was one of the sites that Dino conceded *was* as big as he had pictured. Not only was there a massive open square outside of St. Mark's cathedral, but there was another open area perpendicular to the Square, lined with hotels and cafes. In film of St. Mark's I always noted the pigeons. Evidently, people are encouraged to feed the pigeons in Saint Mark's Square. I think this idea was promoted by a large family of influential cats that lives near the docks. People were doing the Saint Francis of Assisi thing, holding their hands out while the stinking, lousy, flying rats ate out of their hands, and hair, and pockets. Do that in Philadelphia and you are either taken to a mental hospital or get elected to the city council.

While we were walking around, Dino spotted a smallish painting at a sidewalk gallery that he thought his dad might like. He figured he would come back for it later. As we continued to walk, it became apparent there were at least fifty sidewalk galleries in this sinking New Orleans with an accent. Over the next two days, we spent a little time looking for that same picture. When I say a little time, I mean compared to eternity.

One of the myths about Venice is that it smells bad. To our pleasant surprise, Venice did not stink at all. Maybe our timing was good, but we didn't notice any foul odor at all. I have to admit I was a little disappointed because I was curious as to what this bad smell would be like. Kind of like having to test the bad milk and not just taking somebody's word for it.

Since we were in the area we went to see the inside of Dino and Cathy's hotel. It was beautiful and elegant, exactly what you would expect from a classy European hotel (although the lobby area was large and confusing, and it was hard to find the elevators). Everywhere we turned, there were hotel employees looking at me as if they already knew I had no business being in such a nice place. When we encountered these people, Dino would go up to them and tell them not to worry: I was just a loser American acquaintance he had accidentally made eye contact with while I was feeding pigeons in the square, and he would have me out of the building within an hour. I waited for Dino to throw a coat over my head and lead me to their room like a convicted felon.

We made our way up to their room, which was luxurious, although a little on the small side. Dino turned on the TV, on the off chance there was some mid-afternoon Italian porn on, but no luck for him. The room had a nice view, a minibar, and a refrigerator, and the furniture and appointments were very nice. But it had no balcony, so I was satisfied. We could leave.

We went back out, and I found a drugstore. In Europe, antibiotics are sold over the counter, but I have been brainwashed by our American health-care system, so I was too scared to buy any and just got a decongestant for my cold. Along the Grand Canal, we found the famous Harry's Bar, which popularized the official cocktail of Venice, the Bellini—Prosecco or champagne with peach nectar. Harry's Bar in Manhattan actually created the drink, but the Venice location is where it gained its cachet. Inside we could see why. It was a nice room, but the real drama was on the menu, where a Bellini went for about nineteen dollars a pop. That's cachet, pal. A bartender is mixing seven-dollar-a-bottle Prosecco with thirty-five cents worth of peach juice, and people are swilling it down like it's Pabst Blue Ribbon beer. The Bellinis we got at dinner that night were about six bucks. You buy a couple of the nineteen-dollar versions for you and the spouse at Harry's, and the next day you realize you feel like crap, not because you drank peach juice and champagne, but because now you want to buy a pizza and you can't afford mushrooms. That's a tragedy.

We started looking for restaurants in San Marco but were not impressed with the menus at the places on the main streets. The food was pricey, and the menus were more limited than any we had seen the previous two weeks. Eventually, we found ourselves at the Academia Bridge that connected San Marco with Dorsoduro, so we walked over. I was trying to figure out if I could find my way back to our hotel when we came across a little restaurant called Taverna San Trovaso. It looked like the same kind of unpretentious but fabulous places we had enjoyed in Florence and Rome. Plus, it was closed until 7, just like Marione, so we figured this was the spot for us.

The only problem was, I had no idea where we were. Venice was ridiculous: all these weaving little canals and sidewalks, and the address numbers made no sense. It was as though the place was laid out normally hundreds of years ago, and then somebody added water, took a giant spoon, and started stirring. On the Web site, the hotel had two addresses ; one was Fondamenta Gabardino 1675 along the Rio San Barbara. The address the hotel manager gave us was 4823 Dorsoduro, which is not much better; 4823 Dorsoduro is like saying 4823 Kansas. There is only one 4823 in Dorsoduro. OK, I'll buy that, but right next door was 819 Dorsoduro, and that was across the bridge from 123 Elm Street, Your Town, Italy. The next morning I watched little kids trying to walk to school. Most of them gave up after ten or fifteen minutes and stopped to have coffee or become prostitutes. And now I had to not only find the hotel, but then figure out how to get back to the restaurant and to the bridge so Dino could watch a little porn to work up his appetite in time for dinner. I didn't even try to pretend I had a clue. I looked at the sun from different angles, I measured shadows off of tall buildings, I drew chalk maps on the sidewalk, and finally I just took every dead end in sight until we mysteriously found our way to each of the points we needed. We parted at the bridge. Dino said that we would meet back there at 6:45, and that I was to have a much better idea of where the hell we were by then. I told Dino that if he could find his way back to his hotel and then back to this bridge by 6:45, I could find the restaurant. It was 5:15. He looked at me, then he thought for a second, then he told Cathy to go back to the hotel and bring back his tan shorts. He wasn't taking any chances.

Maybe because we had now gone down every dead end in Venice, I had no trouble finding our way back to the hotel and the restaurant. I used a series of landmarks, like the scary bar where I thought we were going to get jumped in broad daylight, and the restaurant where the maitre d' wouldn't make eye contact. This not only helped us find our way, it helped us stay on time. We went back to the room to take a quick shower before dinner. Imagine a shower stall shoved into an airplane bathroom; that was about the scale. I opened the window in the bathroom just to give myself the illusion of space. Then I realized that with the window open, I could put my pants and shirt on without breaking the mirror or flushing the toilet. This was a small bathroom. But we got ready and, feeling refreshed, left to go meet Dino and Cathy.

The evening light was still shining on the canal and the buildings. It made for a great picture, assuming you didn't forget your camera, Peter. But we didn't have much time, because Dino and Cathy were on time. I figured they must have paid a cop to lead them 90 percent of the way there. Of course, Dino might have asked, "Dove Ponte Academia?" But he never would have understood the answer. As they approached the bridge and saw both of us standing there, Dino stopped short, as if he had walked into a wall. Carolyn? On time? It was an Italian miracle. Two nights left on the trip, and Carolyn was on time. At least she didn't spoil him. We walked over the bridge back to Dorsoduro and made it to the restaurant with no trouble. We were third or fourth in line, so there was no problem getting a table. I was reassured by the fact that there were locals in the line. If the locals ate here, it had to be good. Then I thought about how crowded it is at Chili's all the time, and I got nervous. I could tell these were locals by their language. These were native Italians—unless they were Egyptian cotton merchants. They all talk so fast.

Anyway, the doors opened at 7, and we got a table in the front room on the first floor. There was no sense risking exploring for a better spot. Like my dad said, "You can't eat ambience." For twenty years, I thought ambience was a kind of tuna that maybe had mercury poisoning. Anyway, we sat down and the menu was terrific: lots of options, and the prices were at least 30 percent lower than the restaurants we saw in San Marco. Osso buco, scallops, steak, lasagna, white tartufo for desert, it was all *perfetto*. The girls had Bellinis, Dino and I had wine. I figured I had a five-hundred-yard walk home, and only 250 yards of it were along canals, so even drunk there was only a 50% chance of me falling in and drowning. I've never been good at statistics

At about 9 p.m., I noticed that the people who hadn't gotten a table when the restaurant opened were still sitting in the foyer waiting. They didn't seem to mind at all. That was nuts. If I have to wait more than twenty minutes, I get ants in my pants and take off. We finally got up to leave at 10. The people waiting finally got a table and were perfectly fine about it. I guess if you're going to eat this good, you don't mind, but these guys didn't even have a crossword puzzle or a BlackBerry. Amazing.

I had been thinking about gelato all day, but dinner was so good I didn't need anything else, and we retired to our respective hotel rooms for the night. I checked my Blackberry. Dan had sent a note confirming where I would meet Paul, the literary agent on Tuesday morning for coffee. I didn't have the heart to tell him it was all for nothing. Maybe I would catch a break and he would have a stroke and reschedule. Probably not. Carolyn and I shoehorned our way into our room and zonked out, wondering why we hadn't asked Cathy to pick our hotel room.

September 21: According to Dino

I don't know what to expect when we get to Venice, but Cathy obviously does. She pulls out her little notebook and tells us exactly which *vaporetto* (water taxi) to jump on based on her months of blog reading. Between her constant notebook reading and Peter's constant diary writing, (which will hopefully stop soon now that he's given up on the book idea) I feel like I'm on vacation with the Geek Squad. Thank God Carolyn doesn't have the same compulsions. OK, that's the last time I'm sticking up for Carolyn. I just had to get it off my chest. It's off.

I actually feel bad for Pete. He was really into his book idea and then to find out that he didn't have shit must be pretty rough. Imagine finding out that you were plagiarizing a shitty movie. If anything he should have plagiarized the book, which was a hell of a lot better. Whatever. Maybe he'll reconsider one of my suggestions.

The water taxi takes a pretty interesting route through a network of canals to get to our hotel, and I stand up and pull out my trusty Flip video camera to tape the whole thing. Once, when we go under a little bridge, the driver yells back to me to watch my head because there's about eight inches of clearance between the top of the boat and the bottom of the bridge. Unfortunately, he shouts it in Italian, and by the time I can translate it, it's too late. I love it when people watch the video and ask me why I taped the sky for about five minutes.

By the time we get to the pier at our hotel, the Westin Europa, I can almost remember my name, and the ringing in my ears had abated considerably. As we pull up to the hotel, I see that there's a small patio next to the pier where you can gaze across the Grand Canal and see the famous Basilica di Santa Maria della Salute. Well, you could if it wasn't covered by about ninety tons of scaffolding. Today it looks like the outside of the Grecos' hotel room in Florence. The basilica has an interesting history: In the 1600s, the head of the city, let's call him Guido, built the church after the plague hit Venice, because he thought God provided a miracle by stopping the plague after only killing a third of the population. For most people, having a third of the population die wouldn't be a cause for celebration, but not so for Guido. You see, he evidently owed a lot of people a lot of money. So suddenly free from his fiscal responsibilities he did what he figured God would want him to do with his newfound wealth – build another church. I know this is true because Pete Greco told it to me, and Pete Greco knows all about these things.

Several people are sitting on the hotel patio drinking wine and coffee, and I can already see a chair with my name on it. (It doesn't really have my name on it; that's just a figure of speech. Unless, of course, your name is Greco. Then it probably does have your name on it.) Well, the best thing that happens on the entire trip happens right then: we get out of the boat and the Grecos don't. I almost feel bad when we wave to them as the water taxi moves off on the way to their hotel, which is in a different section of Venice called Dorsoduro. I think that means "East Harlem" in Italian. When the Grecos check in, they give Pete a key that's attached to a short chain that's connected to two sticks. Pete jokingly tells the desk guy that it looks like nunchucks. The desk guy laughs and says, "No, of course not." Then with eyes darting from side to side, "but keep it ona you at all times. Even whenna you sleep."

When we check in, it's a whole different story. The guy at the desk asks us to sign in, and he glances at our name. "OK," he says. "Thank you. Enjoy your stay." That's it. No, "Hey, you're Italian just like us!! Welcome home, *paisan!*" Instead he acts like we just wrote down "Harold and Glenda Finkelstein." It's been the same type of reaction everywhere in Italy. Italians view us Italian-Americans like we're Gucci knockoffs. What the hell? If it wasn't for all of us Italian-Americans who the hell would they export all of that olive oil to? They ever think of that? Who'd want all of their Pecorino Romano? The Irish, for God's sake? Without us, their economy crumbles and I'm getting tired of being taken for granted! I'm about to explain this to the entire lobby of "real"

Italians when my wife senses what's coming and pulls me away and guides me to our room.

The room is nice. No view, kinda small, but unlike the Grecos, we don't have to push the bureau in front of the door when we turn in for the night. Cathy is wondering how the Grecos' hotel is, because this is the only thing besides the Vatican tour and getting us all to the Piazza Navona that Carolyn was handling on her own. Unlike Cathy, I'm not concerned. I'm absolutely sure she screwed it up.

We unpack a little, and then about an hour later we all meet up and decide to take a walk and see some of the city. Venice is a very confusing town. Maybe that's because everything is built around the canals, but I think little Italian kids spend the first three years of school memorizing the streets and are told, "Now remember, boys anda girls. Never pay attention to da streeta signs. They're only there to screwa with da toorists." I now understand why the shops always sell the city maps right next to the rosary beads. I try to navigate by landmarks, but that doesn't work too well either. "Let's see, we go past the cheese shop, and then make a left at the store that sells Venetian Carnevale masks, then pass three cheese shops before I get to another mask store." Doesn't work. I'm lost and hungry, and by now I'm thinking of buying a mask at the mask store so I can steal some cheese from the cheese store.

The streets are narrow, and just when we're getting a little claustrophobic, it opens up into a square where there's a church (really?) and a few nice *ristorantes*. This has a totally different feel from Florence, which in turn had a totally different feel from Rome. Here the canals weave in and out of everything, and you're either climbing over them or walking alongside of them, all the while making sure you don't fall into them. It's unlike anywhere else in the world. In some places the gondolas are bumper to bumper, but there are still plenty of them tied up to the docks with their gondoliers sitting around little tables, playing cards, and acting like they could give a shit if you want a ride or not. If you think Italians have attitudes, you gotta see these guys. Even other Italians think these guys have attitudes. Don't get me wrong, they can be friendly—just not when they're working. I'm sure at family reunions they're a barrel of laughs. But the gondolas are pretty expensive, so most Venetians take water taxis, or if they're really on the cheap, they all pile into one little gondola called a *traghetto*, where they have to stand up to save space. Can you visualize this? About fifteen people *standing*, scrunched together in something that resembles a long canoe. They might as well just hand out life vests along with the tickets. I heard that an Albanian was on board once, and he picked his own pocket.

Most of the streets and canals are pretty narrow, so when we finally find Piazza San Marco, we are really surprised. First, because we actually did find it. Second, because the place is huge. It's a tremendous open plaza surrounded by buildings and the Basilica di San Marco. Beautiful sculptures are everywhere, and after ten days in Italy, you almost start taking it all for granted, until you see something like this. A huge tower, the Campanile, is at one end, and you get the feeling that you're in the courtyard of a huge medieval castle. The square is full of people, which makes it ripe for pickpockets. I'm relieved that no one picks my pocket, and even happier that no one sees me grab the telephoto lens from an elderly Japanese gentleman. Only kidding, but I am tempted as I could really use a lens like that. Besides the throngs of people, there are pigeons (or, according to headwaiters in New York City, quail) everywhere. This creates a minor problem for Cathy, because she is deathly afraid of birds. All birds. What makes it even worse is that the pigeons go nuts every time someone throws a piece of biscotti up in the air. I keep Cathy close because I have a sore shoulder and can't throw my leftover biscotti bits very far. Pete says something, but I can't hear him over my wife's incessant screaming. Pete keeps yelling, but I still can't hear him. I'm getting frustrated, as this continues for almost ten minutes (until all of my biscotti is gone).

We meander around the square and check out the wares of many of the street vendors. It's here that I caught on to another scam. I see that paintings of local water scenes are pretty popular with most of the vendors, but a lot of the different vendors have very similar-looking paintings. I can see that although they look like originals (and are priced that way) they're just prints on canvas that someone applied paint to so they appear to be originals. Growing up in New Jersey does have its advantages.

Pete and Carolyn are still trying to reassure Cathy that they won't let me buy another biscotti, and I hear one of them mention dinner. By this time I'm like one of Pavlov's dogs, and when I think of our next meal I start salivating like a Saint Bernard. I swear, the drool coming from the left side of my mouth is almost touching the ground. We agree to meet at a place we heard about that's fairly equidistant from each of our hotels. When we get there, it reminds me a little of Marione. No tourists—just locals, and us, and wonderful, wonderful food. Among other things, I have a lasagna Bolognese, which is very different from the lasagna I know and love. This is more condensed, and, God help me, I don't think it had any ricotta in it. Because of my love for my grandmother's Calabrese-style lasagna, made with tons of cheese and little meatballs, I never order lasagna at a restaurant, but thankfully I make an exception this time. It is absolutely delicious—different, but delicious.

There is a large gathering of people at one long table, and one of them is a big, heavyset (translation: fat) priest who's knocking down plates of pasta and glasses of vino like this is the Last Supper. I'm trying to keep up with the good padre, but in the end it's just no contest. He lets me stay within a couple of forkfuls for a while, toying with me, but then he shifts into another gear, a gear that I had no idea even existed, and he leaves me in a wake of garlic sauce and marinated eggplant. After dinner, Cathy and I work off a course or two as we leisurely walk back to our hotel. The Grecos probably work off all of their dinner, as I'm sure they're running as fast as they can through the dark alleys hitting dead end after dead end on the way to their hotel like two terrified lab rats caught in a maze. Makes me laugh even now just picturing it. Nice job with the hotel selection, Carolyn. Serves her right (*Ti sta bene*) for messing up the other stuff.

Monday, September 22: Peter's Version

Because I got up first, I went downstairs to see what breakfast was like. It was very good. When Carolyn came downstairs, it was clear the charm of Hotel Diphtheria hadn't grown on her. The breakfast attendant couldn't have been nicer. He got us coffee and made sure every item on the buffet was refilled. Carolyn, being Irish, has almost a ceremonial appreciation of tea. So when the Lord of Breakfast brought her hot water and an assortment of tea bags, she relaxed and enjoyed the moment.

After breakfast, Carolyn and I headed over to meet Dino and Cathy near their hotel. On the way we got caught up in a parade. It turned out to be a union march/celebration. I couldn't tell what union it was, but they welcomed us to the parade. If they were on strike, they were pretty happy about it. While in the U.S. they would have been carrying placards, these guys had flags and pennants. Based on the drawings on the flags, it seemed this union was responsible for golden statues of men carrying hammers while walking with lions. You see a lot of both in Italy, so they must be very good. When the parade reached a near-empty square, the marchers seemed to lose interest, and the whole affair broke up for a coffee break. I changed my mind again, someday I want to live in Italy.

Today we went to the famous Murano glassworks. Cathy and Dino found out where to catch a boat that takes you to Murano the island where the world famous glass works were located. I think the deal was, if you bought enough from the glass places, you rode back for free, and if you didn't spend enough, they dumped you in the water while going about thirty knots. When we got off the boat, we were met by a manager of one of the high-profile glass emporiums. There was competition to be the first place you shopped, and this guy met people as they got off the boat and guided them into his facility. He was well-dressed and cosmopolitan, so I was immediately put off by him. Let's call him Ernesto. Clearly, he expected visitors to spend ridiculous amounts of money—except for me. He graciously took Carolyn's hand and warmly greeted her, then did the same with Cathy. He gave Dino a hearty handshake and patted him on the back as they exchanged Italian greetings. Then he looked at me, gave me a two euro coin, and told me to make sure nobody stole the boat while these nice people were shopping. That was embarrassing, but nobody laid a finger on that goddamned boat.

(Note: I had a hard time trying to relate the next piece of the journal without a slew of double entendres. In the end I gave up trying. So the next two paragraphs have built-in rest stops so readers who are so inclined can have their fun and we can move on with the story.)

When we entered the building, we saw a beautiful, ornate glass chandelier hanging from the ceiling (Peter's note: When I read the previous sentence after the trip I actually insulted myself asking, "Are there chandeliers that spring out from the floor?"). Ernesto took us to a room where some of the glasswork was done. He described the furnace and the technique. Two men were sitting by a workbench taking a break. Ernesto looked at them. They looked at Ernesto. It was a staring contest, and they both started making small gestures with their shoulders and hands. But the object of the game wasn't to make somebody laugh first. The object was to get one of the workers to stop his break and demonstrate glassblowing, in order to further induce us to buy something when we got to the store upstairs. It was obvious to the workers that Dino and I weren't going to buy any chandeliers, but Ernesto thought that maybe the classy broads would be game changers. Finally, one of the workers wearily got up and, with Ernesto narrating, took a long cast iron tube, dipped it into some sandy material, and then stuck that end into the furnace. When he pulled it out, it was glowing. (Rest stop one. I'll pause here so Dino and other readers can comment on that last sentence… OK, let's move on.)

After he pulled the tube out of the furnace, he blew on the cold end while twisting it at the same time. This made the melted, shiny stuff at the hot end get bigger and change shape. (Rest stop two. Even I need a break here.) As he turned and blew, the object at the end took on a more-defined figure, and he started using tools to work the material. Now the object was changing color. Ernesto informed us that the color and shape of the final piece was determined by the material that the glassblower used. As the material began to cool, he stopped blowing and focused on playing with the stuff at the other end (Rest stop three.) With a few strategic strokes at the end, he fashioned the blue glob into a horse standing on its hind legs. Even though he was reluctant in the beginning, you could tell the glassworker was pleased with our reaction and the tip I left him. When he was done, he headed out back for a smoke.

Upstairs was room after room of amazing glasswork. Each room was exquisitely laid out, and we could just sense the quality all around us. On display for sale were sets of wine glasses, sculptures, chandeliers, clocks, mobiles, frames, dishes—but no horses up on their hind legs. There was some beautiful stemware, and I saw one blue-green goblet that I thought was especially nice. I looked under the base for the price, and doing a quick euro-to-dollars conversion calculated that this little beauty could be mine for a mere seventy-five dollars. One glass, seventy-five dollars. I looked further and realized that the first one I had picked up was in the low middle range. Some of the wine glasses cost $125 apiece. As we walked through the various rooms, we noticed a woman sitting at a table with a sales representative. She was ordering two twelve-piece sets of the $125 wine glasses as Christmas gifts. That's fifteen hundred dollars for each set—for Christmas presents. And that doesn't factor in that this lady flew to Venice just to do her Christmas shopping. I got a shirt and a stapler that year. Nothing says "out of my league" like seeing somebody price up three thousand dollars worth of glasses while I'm putting down a nine-dollar toothpick holder. Fortunately, there was a gift shop downstairs near the exit where you could buy T-shirts with sayings like, "Some lady spent $3,000 in Venice. I swiped this $3 T-shirt while nobody was looking."

We stopped by a few other glass emporiums as we walked around the island. By now it was mid-afternoon, so we stopped to have lunch. We went to an outdoor pizzeria on one of the canals. As we waited for our food, I looked across the canal and saw an apartment building. Looking up the wall, I saw an old woman with her head out the window smoking a cigarette. She had some underwear drying on a line. I quickly got out my camera and tried to focus in on her, but she just as quickly pulled her head back into her apartment and shut the window. Carolyn thought she might have been embarrassed. I said, "By what, the smoking, the underwear, or staring at us waiting for pizza?" Isn't there an unwritten rule that all inhabitants of a tourist city must make themselves pleasantly available for photographs and stupid questions asked slowly in a loud voice?

Lunch was great: pizza and salad at Café Carvallo. We took our time and went back to the boat. When we got on board, we waved our bags at the pilot, and he didn't charge us. Ernesto wasn't there to point out that we had spent about seventeen dollars, including lunch, so we were home free. It was a great boat ride back. We passed a cemetery. Because of the water level, there is a separate island in Venice for a cemetery. I imagine there's a big push for cremation. The things you don't think of when your city isn't slowly sinking.

We got back from Murano and spent the rest of the afternoon looking for the painting Dino had spotted for his father the day before. I calculated that the time we spent looking for the picture was about the same amount of time we spent waiting for "Where's Carolyn" to get ready to go out, so they canceled each other out, and I kept my mouth shut. That's what a college education teaches you. The search wasn't a total loss: I saw a cute dog and inside a church found a display of stringed instruments from the middle ages. It turned out that the rest of the gang wasn't as enthusiastic about lutes as I was, so our visit to that little display was a quick one. But outside the church where I saw the old instruments, we looked off a few blocks in the distance and saw a tower. It wasn't anything special, but when we looked at it with other closer buildings for perspective, this tower was clearly leaning. Son of a bitch, these leaning towers are a franchise! They've got leaning towers in every major city in freaking Italy. That's why Vincenzo didn't make us stop in Pisa. They have about eleven forums, fifty-five duomos, and leaning towers out the ass—and not one golden arch. Pretty sweet place.

There was no debate about dinner because at about 5:30 Dino said, "So we'll go back to our rooms for a little bit and then have dinner at Taverna Trovaso again. See you guys later." And with that he walked off toward his hotel. Cathy stood there and started to apologize on her husband's behalf. For a second she thought about following us, then she thought about doing some more shopping. Then she realized Dino had the key, so she raced to catch up with him so she could get a shower before Dino used the bathroom.

It's funny how sometimes, after only a brief period of time, a strange place can become familiar. It's funny, but it didn't happen in Dorsoduro. We got over the Academia Bridge and made the same right turn followed by the same left turn, which should have taken us past Taverna Trovaso. Should have. This time it took us over a smaller bridge to a dead end. We turned around and headed back to the Academia Bridge to get our bearings again, but somebody must have moved the bridge, because the next thing I knew, we were in a church. Trying not to panic, I decided to go down every street and alley we came across as fast as we could. This way we could make twenty or thirty mistakes in ten minutes, applying the old joke, "We're lost but making great time." It worked. Without warning we were at the square near our hotel, and we still had seven minutes to shower, get dressed, and find our way back to the restaurant.

Dinner at Taverna Trovaso was great again. When we stuck to our formula of avoiding obvious mainstream tourist traps, we were always rewarded. After dinner, we walked around a little bit and found a little place near the D'Adamos' hotel where we could have dessert and a nightcap. The evenings were beginning to get cooler, so we got pastry instead of gelato. By the end of the evening, we were just staring into space. I was thinking at mach 2 trying to come up with something to tell Paul the next morning. I figured the other three were trying to help me, each reflecting on memorable parts of the trip until Cathy said, "If I don't bring back any of my shoes, everything will fit into the suitcases."

When I got back to our room I went through all of my notes on the trip from beginning to end; looking for an angle. Nothing. It was time for plan B, my excuses. Even there I had trouble coming up with something plausible. Finally, at about two in the morning, I decided honesty was the best policy. When I met Paul in the morning, I would just come clean. I had one good idea; it just happened to be somebody else's.

Monday, September 22: According to Dino

You ever wake up in the middle of the night and open your eyes and see the guy in the hockey mask from *Halloween* staring at you? I think I scream louder than Jamie Lee Curtis, but I'm not sure. Probably woke up half the hotel before I realize it's one of those fucking Carnevale masks that the hotel leaves propped up on my end table. Obviously I can't get back to sleep, because even though I now know that this nightmare isn't real, I come to the realization that in just a few hours I'll be with the Grecos again. Given a choice between the two scenarios, I think I'd go with Michael Myers.

The hotel has a nice little breakfast room, and the wife and I order a couple of lattes and a plate of pastries. While Cathy is still eating, I walk over to the concierge, which in Italian (and I suppose every other language) means "the guy who makes reservations only for places where he gets a kickback." Knowing this, I ask him about getting to Murano, the island famous for glassblowing, which I know is a relatively short boat ride away. He says, "No problem. I makea reservations. How many people and whata time?" I tell him, and he says a boat will meet us at the hotel dock. I ask him how much, and he says, "No charge."

Uh oh. Too good to be true. If the boat ride is free, I know I'm gonna get destroyed at the stores, but what can I do?

We call the Grecos and tell them to meet us in an hour, which they do, and we all head over to Murano on the water taxi. This time the trip is over open water (no bridges), and we manage to make the ten-minute ride without incident. When we get to Murano, we dock at a short wooden pier and are greeted by an older man in a jacket and tie who resembled the late Italian actor, Rossano Brazzi. I think he had his suit jacket draped over his shoulders and is holding his cigarette in that palm-up European way, but that could be my imagination. But I swear he was humming, 'Some Enchanted Evening'.

He greets us like we're old friends (amici) and immediately

leads us into the area where the kilns are. Eventually an old man comes out and blows an unbelievably intricate figure of a horse in about two minutes. What makes it even more amazing is that it's lunchtime, and he's able to do it while simultaneously knocking down a foot-long panini. I ask Rossano if we can buy the horse, and he sticks out his finger and says, "No." I ask him if he's related to a waitress at Marione. He informs me that after the glass is blown, it is put in an oven to allow it to cool slowly, because if they didn't do that with this figure, it will just break anyway.

I feel bad for the horse as it stands there unaware but probably suspecting its fate. I identify with him as Rossano leads us into the showroom. Unbelievably intricate and beautiful chandeliers, glass sculptures, and vases cover almost every square foot. The level of artwork is absolutely mind boggling, and as my wife is oohing and ahhing, I'm checking out the prices, which are completely nuts and I'm hoping that Cathy is not going to force me to take out *another* mortgage on the house so she can buy a sconce. Luckily, even she seems to understand that these things are not in the budget (which totally confuses me as I didn't think she was familiar with the term). Finally we thank Rossano and get ready to leave. This is way too easy however. I'm thinking that this is where I get the sales pitch similar to the vultures back home who try to intimidate you into buying two weeks of time-share in sunny Orlando.

But to my surprise, he just smiles and escorts us to the gift shop. Little do I know that this is where the scam begins. You're so relieved to get out of the showroom unscathed, and you don't want to look like a total cheap bastard to Rossano, especially because you got a free round-trip boat ride, that you feel compelled to buy something here. Prices are high but not insane. So we purchase a few things, thinking that at least we will have a few mementos from Murano, just enough to impress the neighbors. It isn't until months later, when we're strolling through a T.J. Maxx and I see shelves and shelves of "Made in Murano" glass, that I really kick myself in the ass. I could have bought half the store for what I paid for one stinking paperweight. Plus I had to carry the damn things home.

Rossano wants to escort us back to the boat so we don't get a chance to explore the rest of the island and find other, cheaper stores (that don't provide round-trip transportation), but the boat is delayed. This allows us time to grab lunch, shop for a while longer, and catch a ride back to the hotel later. It's another beautiful day, and we find a little trattoria where we can enjoy some pasta and pizza and down a few cold Italiano brewskis. The trattoria, like every other one on the island, sits beside a canal, so we grab a table along the water. Small rowboats tied to the docks sit perfectly still in the noonday sun and I'm actually having a nice time chatting with the Grecos. I'm wondering what's going on with this and recollect that the Mussolini's were said to be charming dinner guests as well.

Just as I start to rationalize my strange behavior, the term "Stocholm syndrome" pops into my head like a big neon sign with the "k" unlit (which is probably why I just misspelled it here). It's that condition where after a period of time you start to develop a relationship with your terrorist captors. That's it! That explains it. But what can I do? I don't know... Escape! I must escape, but for now, just play it cool. Don't panic I tell myself. The time will come.

We hit a few other glass showrooms and then head back to catch the boat. On the ride back I decide that we're going back to Taverna Trovaso for dinner tonight. Some of the others seem disappointed that we're returning to the same place where we ate the night before (even though they admit the food there is wonderful). I'm a reasonable guy, so in the spirit of compromise, I insist that tonight we sit at a different table.

Normally we drink red wine, whatever the house specialty is, but since Venice is right in Prosecco country, we have a couple of bottles of that instead. In France they have a rule that no one can call what they make Champagne unless the grapes are grown in that specific region. Here they do something similar. Only

Prosecco grown here can receive the coveted DOCG designation. Bottom line is, it's really, really good. On the way home we come across a little standing-room-only place that sells pastry and shots. My kinda place. After about thirty minutes of mixing sambuca and canoli, we head back to our respective hotels—we're in a beautiful and elegant establishment on the Grand Canal. Meanwhile the Grecos are in Italy's answer to Motel 6.

I already have a buzz on, but the bar in the hotel looks so damn enticing that I stop for another nightcap, but Cathy decides to head back to the room. Now, at home we have sheets with a dotted line down the middle, and I'm supposed to signal if I'm thinking of changing lanes. Know what I mean? So before Cathy leaves, I give her that suave D'Adamo grin, which is my way of letting her know that she's in store for some reckless driving tonight. One Sambuca somehow turns into four and by the time I get to the room the light's out and she's already in bed. I quickly undress, and although I'm definitely in the mood, I can tell that Cathy isn't. My first clue is she's wearing that string of garlic around her neck that she bought from a street vendor. Second, she has duct taped the "Do Not Disturb" sign to the front of her pajamas. (Where the hell did she get the duct tape? Unless she brought it from home, which would then officially qualify this little action as an obvious case of premeditated spousal abuse.). I'm really pissed, but I have to hand it to my Asian adversary. Well played, my little spring roll. Well played.

Tuesday, September 23: Peter's Version

Paul and I were to meet at a café near the Academia Bridge at 8:00 in the morning. Carolyn would eat breakfast at the hotel and we would catch up at the bridge after the meeting and then go to Cathy and Dino's hotel by 9:30. I walked into the café and spotted the only man sitting by himself and introduced myself. He was very gracious, and also the wrong guy. So I went to the host and got myself seated. At least I would score a point for being the first one there. Paul showed up shortly afterwards and we did the awkward nod and mouthing of each other's names and then shook hands and sat down for formal introductions. The waiter took our breakfast orders and we began a conversation that is indelibly imprinted on my memory; like scribbling on a wedding dress with a Sharpie pen.

Paul: So, Peter, have you enjoyed your trip?

Peter: Absolutely, it's been amazing. Italy is as advertised.

Paul: Are you traveling with your wife or a group?

Peter: Actually I'm traveling with my wife and a circus.

Paul: How's that?

Peter: Well, we're traveling with another couple, Cathy and Dino. Cathy's very nice but Dino…

Paul: You don't like him?

Peter: That's the thing. I love the guy, but he lives in a parallel universe. It's like he's always on acid and can't understand why you're not playing croquet with the marshmallow kangaroo. This whole trip he was busting my balls, pardon my French. Anybody else would have had him whacked. I swear if the Pope went on a vacation with Dino, the Holy Father would have broken eight commandments by the end of the first week, and that's only because the Pope would have a tough time getting laid.

Paul (laughing!): Sounds like an interesting guy.

Peter: The Pope? I don't know…strikes me as a little holier than thou. Paul laughed some more so I decided to start working in an excuse or two.

Peter: You can't imagine how hard it was to write an outline these past two weeks. Dino was disappointed when he discovered he had misread a guidebook and learned that the Vatican Museum had a Hall of *tapestries* and not a hall of *Pastries.* Each of us had assignments for the trip. Mine was to learn all of the history of the places we visited. Dino would point to a car and say, "What year Fiat is that Pete?" When I didn't know he would say, "Did you study any of the fucking history of this country?"

Paul: What was Dino's job?

Peter: He said he would learn the language.

Paul: How did he do?

Peter: Pretty well, if you consider the fact that the only word he knows in English is "fuck". He's an idiot savant curser, always knows the exact way to work "fuck" into a conversation. So, I guess the fact that he learned thirty-five words in Italian is pretty good.

Paul: Did the wives have assignments too?

Peter: Yes, Cathy was actually the real travel agent for this trip. She found the hotels in Rome and Florence, arranged for two full-day guided tours, and made sure we could get horse tranquilizers for Dino in every city we visited. She did a great job.

Paul: And what was your wife's job?

Peter: Dino didn't trust her with anything so he let her arrange a guided tour of the Vatican since he's not Catholic and we are.

Paul: How did that go?

Peter: Not good. Dino says it's the first time he actually had a net loss of knowledge from an educational experience.

Paul: How could a professional tour guide be that bad?

Peter: We have some of our best people working on that. Fortunately the tour ended near cocktail hour so Dino went easy on me…

Paul: But your wife arranged the tour, not you, right?

Peter: Paul, you don't understand, everything is my fault. Bad tour? My fault. Rain? My fault. Bay of Pigs? My fault.

Paul: Was it like this all day, everyday?

Peter: No, he took a break during meals, unless the restaurant sucked

Paul: Your fault?

Peter: Thank God the food is so good here.

Paul: Did you ever get credit for anything?

Peter: One day in Tuscany our tour guide almost got us all killed in a horrible car crash. Dino started to blame me, but couldn't think of any way it could have been my fault. Then he got pissed at me because he got frustrated trying to find a way to blame me.

Paul: Peter, this is great stuff. I can really see it working as a book.

Peter: (Stunned) Huh?

Paul: You've really come up with something original here

Peter: Huh?

Paul: Have you figured out how you'll express Dino's point of view yet?

Peter: Huh?

Paul: I mean, it would be good to let the reader get inside Dino's head. What format are you thinking of?

Peter: Huh?

Paul: What format? Are you writing a narrative? Will you do it first person?

Peter: (In shock) …I…uh…have been keeping a journal…

Paul: That's a great idea. Has Dino been keeping a journal too?

Peter: Uh…he wrote something down last Friday. I think it was name of a salami exporter.

Paul: Well, you'll need to figure that out. Obviously the relationship between you two is the lynchpin so you need to figure out how to incorporate it.

Peter: Huh?

Paul: Yes, I like what you've come up with here. There aren't too many books that pull off the "buddy" concept without it being too one-sided. I think the give and take you're talking about is pretty cool. The styles are so different, it's almost like reading two different books with one theme. Add Dino's point of view and I think you have a sellable book. Really unique. Here's my card. I figure it will take you guys about three or four months to finish up a good draft. Have it professionally edited and I'll take a look at it personally. Send me an e-mail me in a couple of months to let me know how it's going. I think I we can both make a little money with this. You'll have to do a lot of PR work too, by the way. That's a big piece of this business now. You'll have to plug it together, book signings; use any connections you both have in the media to get the maximum exposure. I gotta run and meet my wife and kids. It was great meeting you. We'll talk soon.

Peter: …Buddy concept?…oh uh thanks very much. I'm very… excited. By the way, Paul, have you ever seen the movie *Under the Tuscan Sun*?

Paul: Yeah, but I liked the book better. Why?

Peter: Oh, nothing…thanks again, I'll be in touch in a couple of weeks

Paul: Okay, enjoy the rest of your trip. Ciao

Peter: Chow

Paul left and I sat at the table in stunned disbelief, unconsciously eating all the food he hadn't finished. What just happened? I was telling him why I didn't have an idea for a book because of Dino and the next thing I know I had a book; *with Dino!* All this time I was looking for a subject for a book on a trip to Italy and it turns out to be Dino? But wait. What was I thinking? I now have to ask Dino to write a book with me. What if he said no? I would be walking away from a chance to get professionally published. Oh my God, what if he said yes? I really couldn't decide which answer I preferred. Maybe the best thing to do was to try and get Paul to let me write the book by myself and create Dino's part. Or maybe just give up the whole idea.

Carolyn was waiting for me at the bridge. My expression must have reflected how conflicted I was because she had a sympathetic look on her face.

Carolyn: So, how did it go?

Peter: You won't believe it. I was all ready to tell him I had nothing, but before I could, he asked me how the vacation went. I started describing the trip so far, with all the things Dino said and did. He thought I was describing the book I was going to write and loved it.

Carolyn: Oh my God, that's unbelievable! That's hilarious! You're going to write a book! That's so exciting!

Peter: Well, maybe

Carolyn: What do you mean "maybe"?

Peter: The guy said it was a good idea provided I also include Dino's side of the story. If I want to write this book, I have to write it with Dino.

Carolyn: Oh, honey, I'm so sorry.

Peter: Thanks

Carolyn: I'm sure there are other books you can write.

Peter: Thanks, do you think there's any way I could actually write a book with Dino?

Carolyn: Hon, you are very intelligent and a good guy and a hard worker. But, no, there's no way you could do it. Not without losing your mind.

Peter: I was trying to think of a way it would work. I mean I've been on vacation with him for two weeks, right?

Carolyn: Yes, with Italy, Cathy and I to dilute the effect. This has been Dino on his best behavior.

Peter: You're right. Listen when we see them, I'm just going to tell him the book is a no go and leave it at that.

Carolyn: You know he's going to give you a hard time about it right?

Peter: Yeah, but I've built up my resistance a little bit over the last couple of weeks. Let's go before we're late, Where's Carolyn.

We met Dino and Cathy outside of their hotel. We were right on time, but Dino gave no quarter, "Where's Carolyn, what happened? Did Pete tell you you were supposed to be here a half hour ago?" Cathy smacked Dino on the arm and asked me how the meeting went with the literary agent. I told her it was a no go and that I was disappointed. Dino said, "That's about what I expected. Let's get going." For our last day we walked through San Marco to the Rialto Bridge on the Grand Canal and over to the San Croce District. This district is actually connected to Dorsoduro, but it would have taken us weeks to find it that way. The streets in San Marco were swirly affairs, but much less confusing. San Croce is a packed little area not far from the train station. There were a number of "delicacies" there that you don't find at the Piggly Wiggly back home. For example, there was a huge fish market, almost like a flea market with dozens of tables set up under a roof, but all with fresh seafood. I'm not sure why we walked by every table. All we did was make "yucking" noises, and every time we turned around there was something more yuck-worthy. We started with fish that were so fresh they still had the look of shock on their faces, like, "Are you kidding me? This is a net? You mean I just got cauuuuuuught?!" Then there was squid complete with ink. Some of the stuff I couldn't even recognize, like a slimy, giant squid, but with legs. That turned out to be the owner's wife. Very nice lady; squished when she walked.

Amidst all of the produce and fish markets there was a horsemeat butcher who actually had a picture of a great stallion drawn on the shop window. And it was crowded. I don't see how you can look at a drawing of a beautiful horse in the window and then go into the shop and say I'll have a pound and a half of that guy in the picture. I'm clearly no vegan, but this bothered even me. We got close enough to take a picture and kept on going.

There were a host of stores in the area, and I bought a sweater. I swear it's a man's sweater, although nothing about it or the store would give you that impression. It was black and had a zipped-up collar, and this would be the last chance I'd have to buy something, and Carolyn insisted on paying for it. I must say it was pretty brave of me to show Dino that sweater. It was not a manly sweater. I only wear it whenever I watch *The Notebook* or just need a good cry.

Other than shopping, there wasn't a whole lot to do or see in San Croce. We went up about five different streets, all of which seem to dump us back to the same spot. About the fourth time around we figured that was enough and headed back to the bridge and San Marco. We got lunch in a pizzeria called Trattoria Ai Nanetti Sotoportega. Dino will have to translate that for you. I think it means "restaurant that will give you the winds." It sure seemed that way for Dino.

By the time we had walked off our lunch, it was 3 p.m. We had started the day early, so we decided to go back, start packing, and take a nap. We got to the point where we were deciding what could be left behind. My poncho from Cinque Terre, the guidebook we borrowed from Carolyn's sister (we would buy her a replacement when we got home), all the silverware and glasses we "absentmindedly" took from the places we'd been, and all remaining snacks were jettisoned. Still, I could hear the stitching on my backpack starting to give way. As it was, I would have to wear four shirts and two pairs of shoes on the plane.

Before dinner it was time to go for broke and have a gondola ride. It was around 6:30, so the sun was starting to set, making it the perfect time for a romantic ride—but we went anyway. About forty gondolas were waiting for us everywhere we looked. We picked a dock, and the gondolier shop steward loaded us up on Nunzio's classic black job with the red cushioned seats. Nunzio made a couple of things clear up front. First, his gondola cost about forty thousand dollars, so don't mess it up. Second, he expected a good tip. Third, he would tell us about Venice, but only what he felt like telling us. Of all the gondolier pilots in all the canals in all of Venice, we got the one who was perfectly matched to us. Several great exchanges made the ride memorable:

Dino: "So, Nunzio, are you going to sing for us?"

Nunzio: "No."

Dino: "Come on, all the gondola pilots sing."

Nunzio: "Only the bad ones."

Dino: "But I want to hear you sing."

Nunzio: "I don't sing."

Dino: "But I'm paying for the ride."

Nunzio: "You pay for the *ride.*"

Dino: "Pete, the gondolier's going down."

And:

Peter: "What's that building over there?"

Nunzio: "Some kind of church … I think."

And:

Dino: "So we were told that Venice really smells bad, but it seems OK. Did they clean it up?"

Nunzio: "This is the land of Pinocchio."

Dino: "You mean you don't want to lie?"

Nunzio: "Your Mr. Bush and Mr. Obama are very nice men."

And:

Peter: "Nunzio, could you take our picture?"

Nunzio: "No, I do the boat, you take the picture."

Peter: "But I'd like a picture of the four of us."

Nunzio: "When we get back."

Peter: "OK, thanks."

Nunzio: "When we get back, you get out of the boat; maybe somebody will take your picture."

Once we shut up, Nunzio was very entertaining, telling us that the land was still sinking, and where Maria Callas stayed when she was in Venice. It was a great ride and very relaxing. I think Dino liked the fact that Nunzio was a smart ass.

The ride was so relaxing and everybody was so at ease that I decided what the hell, why not tell Dino what really happened with Paul that morning.

Peter: Dino, so let me tell you what really happened this morning with the Literary agent.

Dino: Yeah, I thought you were holding back, so I was being nice.

Peter: That was nice?

Dino: So, what did he say when you told him that somebody already wrote the book you want to write?

Peter: He offered me a chance to write a book.

Dino: He wants you to write the same fucking book?

Peter: Nope. He wants me to write a book about trying to write a book when traveling with you.

Dino: Huh?

Cathy: (Snickering) That's funny

Dino: Huh?

Peter: I was going to tell him that I didn't have anything, but then I just started talking about the trip. He thought it was hilarious

Dino: Wait, you're not that funny. What was so hilarious?

Peter: You, mostly

Dino: Me? What kind of bullshit did you feed this guy?

Peter: Just the facts

Dino: The facts? That can't be good for me. So you get to write a book.

Peter: Nope, that's the bad news. I get to write a book, only if I write it with you.

Cathy: Oh my God!

Peter: I've been writing a journal to give me ideas for the book. At night when I tried to come up with a book idea all I had were the usual sites and tour stuff, and you. The publisher thinks if we add your perspective it would make a great book.

Dino: So without me, you got no book. Hmmm, I'll have to give this some thought. Why didn't you tell me this in the first place this morning?

Peter: I was waiting for a romantic setting

Dino: Did he indicate he might like a book just by me?

Peter: No, I painted a pretty accurate picture of you so that's not happening. He just thought your version would make the whole thing…unique

Dino: Well, that's not surprising. Hey, this might be fun, Pete. Why don't we do it? You write the stuff, send it to me and I'll fix it.

Peter: I don't think so, Dino

Dino: Well, you're not going to try to write things from my point of view, are you?

Peter: Dino there aren't enough drugs in the western hemisphere for that. Have you kept any notes from the trip?

Dino: Some, yeah

Peter: Written notes?

Dino: I don't need to write notes, Petey, it's all up here (tapping his head with his forefinger)

Peter: Perfect. I think that's what Paul is counting on…

Carolyn: You know what might work? Each of you write your own book separately and just smush the two of them together after, or let the publisher smush them together.

Dino paused, which of course meant he was having trouble finding fault with the idea. Cathy suggested we also include her and Carolyn's accounts as well. That idea was shot down immediately. Adding an objective perspective would be of no value to this disaster. The rest of the gondola ride was quiet; Dino and I thinking about the book, Cathy and Carolyn just enjoying the silence.

After the ride, we broke our non tourist-trap rule by going to a restaurant on one of the big squares. Unbelievably, I did not write down the name of this last restaurant we ate at in Italy. I can remember clearly where it was, on the big square around the corner from the Academia Bridge. We walked in the door and down a long corridor. My cold was in full bloom, and because we had to get up early the next morning, I ordered the bland with nothing sauce. Everybody else seemed to enjoy their food, but there was no table-banging or eye-rolling like at the other great places. We were tired, ready to go home with what was now an 800 pound *literary* gorilla.

After dinner we walked back to Saint Mark's Square, where we enjoyed one last nice surprise to the trip. Outdoor cafes lined two opposite sides of the square, which extended out toward St Mark's for about 150 yards. There were about six of these cafes, and each one had an orchestra. Each orchestra was a little different from the others, but all of them had at least one violin and a piano. Some of them played show tunes, some played pure classical, and some played a mix. In the dim light, my fabulous camera made the orchestras look like out-of-focus giant insects. Fortunately, Dino got a couple of good pictures. What a great way to end the night, and the vacation.

Our flights the next morning were at different times, and we wouldn't see each other at the airport, so we said our good-byes near the D'Adamos' hotel. Remember what I said about how you form a bond with people after spending a couple of days with them? We had spent two weeks with Dino and Cathy, morning, noon, and night. We shared train rides, long walks, tours, broiling heat, rain, sore backs, gas, and now the prospect of writing a book. Now we were saying good-bye after the most eventful vacation any of us had ever had. I'll never forget the last exchange:

Peter: "Well, guys, this has been an amazing couple of weeks..."

Dino: "Yeah, OK Grecos, see ya later."

And with that, Dino went inside to watch Italian porn and get some sleep.

Tuesday, September 23: According to Dino

It's our last night in Venice and our last night in Italy. Usually when I'm on vacation, by the end of the trip I'm ready to get home, but not this time. I could do another week, no problem. I'm getting pretty depressed, but in an attempt to cheer myself up, I remind myself that I'm not just leaving Italy, I'm also leaving the Grecos. It seems to work a little.

Cathy has made arrangements that we are to meet them at the Rialto Bridge at 10 a.m. I hate leaving details to anyone else. Why? Because no one else gets it right. Like this time, when no one knows which side of the Rialto Bridge we're supposed to meet on. This means that Cathy stays at the foot of one side of the bridge while I continuously make round-trips to see if the Grecos are on the other side. If I've neglected to mention it, this is a big freaking bridge. So I continue this round-trip voyage until I know every shopkeeper who has a store on the bridge by name, weight, and political affiliation. What makes it worse is the Grecos are late— again. When they finally arrive, Carolyn starts a bullshit story about how they got caught in a union parade. Now I ask you, how the hell do you get caught in a parade? (It took the whole damn vacation, but some of you are finally starting to come around to my side about now, aren't you?)

We decide to see the fish and produce market, which means we all have to go back over the bridge—again: "Hello Carlo. How's it going, Emilio? Come stai, Luigi? Carmella, looking good. Ciao Bruno, how's the daughter? Donna," I say, shaking my finger at her, "stop that you little nimrod."

Finally, we're on the other side.

The fish and produce market consists of a bunch of tables and stores that sell, you guessed it, fish and produce. Ordinarily this wouldn't be something I would get excited about. I mean, seriously, how different does an Italian clam look compared to an American clam? But I have to admit, this is a hundred percent better than South Philly. And it smells 5,000 percent better. I pass one place where a really hot Italian woman is cleaning scungilli. In America, hot women are too stuck up for that kind of thing. They're usually legal secretaries or they work in retail. They don't make any money, but for some reason, cutting up raw fish is beneath them. This chick has it going. She's hot and is good with a knife. A very highly prized combination in North Jersey.

We bounce around the market for a while, and I see my wife eyeing a few other strings of garlic in case the one she's already bought starts to fade. Most people think that Asians are really smart. Not this time. Keeping an Italian guy away with garlic is like trying to ward off a bull shark with chum. She later tells me that she heard that it kept vampires away and assumed it would work on all forms of evil. Nothin' but net—the little kung pao chicken scores again.

Speaking of Asians, we start heading back to the bridge, and I look around and immediately start to panic. A busload of Asian tourists are milling about, and I can't find my wife. I tried to remember what color top she had been wearing but can't. I start running through the crowd, grabbing every dark-haired, five-foot-three-inch woman I see. In other words, all of them. Twice I think the one I grab is my wife and start telling her how relieved I am, when they suddenly start yelling at me in Mandarin or some other citrus-based dialect that I can't understand, and I have to resume my frantic search. Finally Cathy comes strolling over to me like nothing has happened. At least I think it's Cathy. I say slowly in a halting tone, "Hi, honey." She just nods. I think it's her, but I have to make sure. "Say, baby, did you speak with our son *Nicholas* today?" She says, "No." I'm not sure if that proved anything. I feel like a mother walrus on one of those Aleutian Islands trying to recognize its offspring by smell, but I'm starting to come down with a freaking cold and it's not working (which also probably explains why the fish smell good). I'm ready to ask her who won the World Series last year when Carolyn walks over and they start gabbing. I wait a second to see if Carolyn gives her a quizzical look, but everything seems to be fine. So, thankfully, I have the right girl. But you know what's really weird? When we got home, she started going through all the rooms of our house like she'd never seen them before. And call me crazy, but I swear her cooking has improved.

When we leave Pete stops at a clothing store and buys another metrosexual sweater. Strike two. One more and I'm going to stop taking showers with him. I was starting to wonder about Pete. Especially since we eventually found that pair of Cathy's panties, but my spare pair of boxers is still missing. Good thing this is our last night.

We finally reach the Rialto Bridge again: "Ciao Donna. Rocco" (I don't like Rocco). "Come stai, Andrea. Fabio, how's it hanging?" (Not really crude. Fabio owns a sausage shop). "Hey, paisan!" (Can't remember his name). Aaaaaand we're over the bridge.

We decide to head back to our hotels so we can freshen up (translation: go to the bathroom, take a quick nap, and then surf for porn while Cathy gets ready). This sounds like an agreeable plan, so with a quick nod, I grab the hand of the woman I'm pretty sure is my wife, and we're off. (While we're at the hotel I get lucky, so now I'm almost positive this isn't my wife, but you didn't hear that from me.)

The sun is setting, and the Grecos and Stepford Cathy tell me that since this is our last night in Venice we have to go on a gondola ride. My job is to negotiate with the gondoliers. Usually my style would be to act like I could care less if I take a ride or not, but I'm not used to dealing with guys who act like they could care even less if they give me a ride or not. I'm going back and forth with the head coach of the gondola team trying to negotiate a price, but I never really mastered the Italian number system. (It's still a deeply shrouded mystery to me, like the metric system).

So anyway, my ignorance has me negotiating at a distinct disadvantage, and I think I finally ended up paying more than they originally asked for. I think that because as soon as we agreed on a price, the gondolier says something to the other gondoliers, and they all start laughing. Shit. I'm still fuming when we all pile into the gondola with our pilot, Nunzio. Most gondolas look the same: black, heavily lacquered, with bright red upholstered seats. People think they are so romantic but I think they look like floating coffins.

Nunzio is pretty good, although all I have to compare him to is a New York City cabbie. I ask him if this is Cash Gondola, and he just looks at me. I say, "You know, like the Cash Cab." He just looks at me. I say, "Where the driver asks you questions and you guess the answers." He just looks at me. I say, "The driver pays you money when you guess right." He says, "How bout I aska you stuff, and when you don' knowa the answer, you pay me?" I just look at him.

Despite everything the ride is really pretty cool and probably worth whatever I paid (but not sure since I still don't know exactly what I did pay). We pass the Peggy Guggenheim Museum which is done in a Baroque style and covered with gold mosaic tile. As the sun sets, it constantly changes color. We pass other beautiful buildings as well, but it's the small details that I like the most. Like the creeping vines that flow down from wrought iron balconies, the ornate painted doors that are at or even below water level, and the weathered brick walls that show decades of paint or plaster that gives way to other coverings, ultimately going back hundreds of years of wives saying, "You know I don't think I like that color." Nunzio won't sing—maybe because his name is Nicola and I keep calling him Nunzio—so I turn on my iPhone, and everybody we pass applauds because they think he sounds exactly like Tony Bennett. I'm enjoying the ride, but that's Pete's cue to transition into his Oprah Winfrey mode. He's asking Nunzio so many questions that he almost gets us lost. Nunzio tells us that the City of Venice brought in a slew of engineers who determined that they had to drill through most of the foundations and set new pilings in order to stabilize the city. That, evidently, was the worst thing they could have done, and the city has been sinking ever since.

The original engineers six centuries ago obviously knew a hell of a lot more than they do today. One of Nunzio's answers gets us all to chuckle: I ask him something about Italian politicians, and he says, "Hey, this is the land of Pinocchio." Meaning everybody lies.

Evidently this includes my friend, Peter Greco, because he finally comes clean about what happened with his meeting with the literary agent. Turns out the guy fell in love with Pete's description of me and wants me to write my own version of the trip. Either that or no deal. In other words Pete sucks on his own and without me, no book deal. I don't know about writing a book but I couldn't have written this script any better. Pete needs me and I couldn't be happier. I let him stew while I make believe that I haven't made up my mind yet, which I obviously have. A book deal would make both of our dreams come true. He gets to tell people that he's a published writer and I get to write the trip off. Sweet.

The sun has set. We head to a nice local family restaurant off of, you guessed it, another little square. It is called Osteria al Schiavoni. This is our last meal in Italia, and it doesn't disappoint. We have four courses: antipasto, various pastas, veal and pounded steak dishes, and grappa (which I now consider a course). When we finally leave, we can't bring ourselves to just head back to our hotels, because that would be admitting that the trip was over. Instead we take another walk to Saint Mark's Square. It's dark now, but the whole square is romantically lit by small lights along the arched walkways (the Procuratie Vecche and the Procuratie Nuove) that run along two opposite sides of the square. A couple of restaurants have small orchestras playing outside, and the music carries beautifully through the square. It's an Italian version of a battle of the bands. I love the United States and have been to almost all of our major cities, but where the hell can you find anything that compares to this? In fact it's obvious there isn't another country in the world that can match the kinds of things we've seen throughout this vacation. We walk slowly back to our hotel, still trying to put off the inevitable until we can't any longer, and finally say our good-byes to the Grecos since we won't get a chance to see them tomorrow. Hopefully they're well rested, because they'll have to run from here. Great trip. God willing, we'll all be back.

We're heading from the train station to our hotel in Venice on a "vaporetto" (small motor boat). After about three concussions you learn to sit the f*@# down!

*Half of Venice is under Construction. Here they're
putting luxury boxes in a Cathedral*

A horsemeat butcher shop in Venice. As you can see from the window, it's been endorsed by the horse's head from The Godfather. The couple inside went in thinking the shop sold food for ponies. Ten minutes later they ran out screaming. I'll never listen to "Mustang Sally" the same way again.

We couldn't get a Gondola ride until the
guy in the sunglasses went Fish

*Dino is negotiating with the Gondola Boss. It was a great match.
Dino kept tipping the boat with his foot and the Gondola
Captain got progressively more seasick. When he finally threw
up, Dino agreed to pay full price and they called it a draw.*

EPILOGUE

"I am not allowed to play my ocarina around the house."

Wednesday, September 24: Peter's Version

We got up early and made our way downstairs and back out to the dock where we had arrived in Venice a few days ago. The water taxi showed up on time. One of the big surprises of this whole trip was the level of efficiency in Italy. We had been led to believe there was little concern for schedules and precision. I had developed enough excess stomach acid to etch the Gettysburg Address on a hubcap thinking we would be late for everything. That's why I was getting up at 5 in the morning to catch a noon train. But such was not the case. Score one for the land of my father's father.

The boat ride to the airport was great, although it did feel odd to get off a boat and start tugging our bags up to an international airport. No circling to find a parking space. When we flew home from Spain a few years before, the security force made us go into a room and empty our suitcases and then rifled through our things for ten minutes. The potential humiliation for that experience is off the charts. In Venice they only asked if we were carrying anything dangerous. I told them no, but I did describe Dino and told them he was coming through in a couple of hours transporting cold cuts in his socks. That is a danger to anybody.

As we sat on the plane waiting to take off, we were commenting on how great the trip was, and we again asked ourselves why. That's a little odd if you think about it. Why would you ask yourself? Why not just tell yourself? Can you be caught off guard by asking yourself a question you weren't expecting? And why would two people ask themselves the same question at the same time? That's just weird. Anyway, we had decided as a foursome that we didn't want to cram the vacation with more things to do than there was time to do them. The priority, as we said, was to relax, and absorb Italia. And it worked. But for Carolyn and I there was one more ingredient. For two weeks, neither of us watched so much as five minutes of television. What could be more entertaining than the Dino show?

There was drama, comedy, music, political commentary, his version of history, wildlife—anything you might watch for a little diversion, he provided. And Cathy was like a diverting human-interest story stuck between a report on a house fire and sports.

We had more luck figuring out the in-flight entertainment system on the way back, but I passed on the food. The shock of going from authentic Italian cuisine to the best the airlines could offer wasn't worth the risk.

Shortly after we got home, we started going through the pictures and reliving the trip. The D'Adamos had one of their sons put together a slide show that had the pictures moving into and out of view to classical music, like a professional multimedia exhibit. We had nine envelopes of five-by-seven pictures that eventually stuck together because I would look at them while eating Oreos. Carolyn and I went through the whole two weeks chronologically, using the photographs and my little notebooks to guide us. At first, we would look at a picture and recall what it was we liked about that particular spot, but after the twelfth time I stopped to refer to my notes for accuracy, we agreed I should shut up for a while.

At this point I was ready to start writing. In short order, I finished a rough draft of an introduction and the first few days' worth of journal entries and sent it to Dino. Dino read it and replied with his version as well as an offer to pay for the psychoanalysis for which he felt my version expressed a dire need. Both of us felt we had some pretty good material; it just had to be organized in a way that made it easy to read. After a painful trip down the tortuous path of Dino's logic, we finally agreed the only reasonable thing to do was to put the two tales under one roof, intertwining each other's daily accounts. But Dino decided it would be better to not see my version first. This way the reader gets two pure, distinct views, or, as Dino put it, "They can decide for themselves that my stuff is better." We proceeded this way and came up with the finished product you now hold.

When most people think of highlights from a trip, they think of things like museums, or natural wonders, or maybe a restaurant. We had a lot of that, too, but most of our highlights were insults, pointing out each others' weaknesses, and double entendres.

That's probably why we aren't invited to go on vacations with other people; they're afraid they'll come home clinically depressed.

When I looked at the pictures from Trevi Fountain taken on the day we arrived, the first thought that came to me was Dino looking at the fountain and saying, "That's it? I mean it's nice, but is this the whole thing? They got bigger fountains in Newark." I pointed out to Dino that in Newark it's not a fountain, it's a busted fire hydrant. How many people could look at a universally admired landmark like the Trevi Fountain and immediately compare it to something in New Jersey?

I looked at the pictures we took strolling through the streets of Rome. Dino loved the Italians' stylish fashion sense, and clearly he decided not to compete or blend in. I mean, the guy wore a Rutgers University Polo shirt and shorts everyday. At night he would dress up and put on a Seton Hall Polo shirt and shorts. No slave to fashion is our friend Dino. That is a little bit harsh, I realize. Especially coming from a guy whose body is so lumpy he is physically unable to keep a shirt tucked in for more than five minutes. I could have the tails of a shirt sewn to my kneecaps and it would still be halfway out of my pants before I tied my shoes. It couldn't be because I buy "off label," could it?

If there was one thing that stuck with me after we returned, it was the priorities of the Italians versus our own. Dino noticed it first: less stuff. Shortly after we got home, we had to buy a new car for Carolyn, because hers was coming off a lease. She asked if just this once she could get a car she saw other people driving. To me that meant Honda, Toyota, etc. To her that meant BMW 325i convertible. We compromised and bought the BMW, because it was on sale. That "It's on sale" logic is ridiculous. They have sales on private jets, too, but it doesn't mean you start building a hangar in the backyard. When Vincenzo was driving us around in his shrunken, mini-SUV, he told us what it cost to live in Florence for a year: about twenty-eight thousand Euros. At the time, that was about thirty-eight thousand dollars. For that you could pay rent on an apartment, pay your bills, and live very comfortably. How? Because the Italians don't absolutely have to have all of the stuff that we absolutely have to have, like big cars, big flat screen TVs, big houses, etc.

When Dino pointed out how much better the Italian quality of life was, I nodded enthusiastically. The girls pretended not to hear and refused to make eye contact. I remember at lunch in Cinque Terre telling Dino he was right—this is the life. If you live in a place like this, all you need is a little forty-hour-a-week job to cover the basics. I asked Carolyn if she agreed. She asked me to pass the bread. Dino asked Cathy if she would enjoy the simple life in a place like Florence. She told Dino he had crumbs on his shirt. A couple of times we talked about returning to Florence and renting a place for a longer vacation. Dino said that if he could be sure he wouldn't see me first thing in the morning, or maybe until mid-afternoon, and some days not at all, he would love it. We decided to look at posted rentals outside real estate offices. Dino and I priced up little three-bedroom apartments, maybe with a patio. Carolyn and Cathy looked at villas with swarthy groundskeepers. So maybe the ladies didn't come to exactly the same conclusion on what was essential to a high quality of life. We did agree that not working sixty-five hours a week was a good thing.

Over lunch in Venice, I asked Dino what he would be doing at this time of day at home. He said he would probably be asking Cathy why he agreed to go on a vacation with the Grecos. I asked him if at any point during the trip he was actually glad we were with him. He told me I had crumbs on my shirt.

If you are thinking about taking a trip to Italy, Rome, Venice, and Florence are among the most popular destination cities, and with good reason. There are some essential things to build into your itinerary. For example when we landed in Rome, taking a shower and a nice little nap before dinner was perfect. Number two, have a casual meal the first night; put the priority on relaxing and getting in a vacation frame of mind. We stayed just north of the Colosseum area, and the neighborhood restaurants are the way to go. Whenever possible we ate outside, and there was never an issue with bugs, or people, intruding on the meal. You might want to scout out the best places for gelato and biscotti before dinner so you don't waste valuable desert time looking for one later. Number three; the classic sights don't disappoint. The Colosseum, the Pantheon, and all the rest are as spectacular as you'd expect.

The scale of these facilities is unexpected, especially when you consider the technology they didn't have and the condition these buildings are in after hundreds, maybe thousands of years. You might want to study up on their history in advance, or get a guided tour, unless the guide is a twenty-eight-year-old dude named John. We chose to make up facts about the places as we went along, and while that probably led to a less fulfilling visit, we managed to keep each other amused.

Try to pace your shopping and focus on the value you will get from an item after you've been back home for a few months. For example, I am not allowed to play my ocarina around the house anymore, so beyond its sentimental value, it might not have been a wise purchase. When you pack for the trip, you could reserve enough space for gifts and souvenirs you anticipate getting, or you might want to take the D'Adamo approach and simply buy everything you see and then shop for a new suitcase big enough to hold it all.

Rome is more spread out than the other two cities we visited, but still, you can walk almost everywhere. We took a cab to the train station and a bus to the Vatican, but everything else on the "must-see" list is pretty easy to get to on foot, even when you add in an extra twenty minutes for getting lost.

Florence is much more compact than Rome. Since you can see a lot of Florence in one or two days, you can make time for rewarding day trips to places like Tuscany, Chianti, or Cinque Terre. Our tour guide offered to take us to Pisa but indicated we would get out of the car, look at the tower, and then get back in the car. Dino figured it would be easier to just get loaded, and then all of the towers would be leaning, so why bother? We agreed. If you are looking for overpriced souvenirs, the stores in some of the smaller towns are every bit as good a place to shop as the big cities. But we found some real bargains in the non-clothing category in towns like Greve, Castellina in Chianti, and Lucca. And the food in these places was terrific as well. What we really liked about Florence was that there was such a variety of things to see in such a compact area. Boboli Gardens has art, nature, and, like Villa Borghese, no booze, but is still worth a half day. In Florence you can walk from a formal garden to a world-class museum in five minutes. *You* can. Dino won't.

In Venice we felt we were winding down but still got exhilarated walking around and exploring. We had no choice because there are no straight lines in Venice. When we got home, everyone we talked to about the trip would ask, "Did Venice stink?" What a horrible reputation to have; people around the world asking if your city smells bad. I didn't think it smelled bad at all. Then again, I've been on the Metro in Barcelona, so maybe my olfactory equipment is no longer functioning properly. Venice is a good two- or three-day visit, but it makes for a longer flight home to the U.S. than Rome or Florence. Unless you have a couple of drinks or an Ambien prescription, in which case it's juuuusst right.

When our son got married months after the trip, Dino and Cathy stayed with us for a couple of days, and we talked about planning another vacation. Dino said he was no longer drunk from the wedding reception, so it wasn't the time to discuss another vacation with the Grecos. Undeterred, I asked what other places he would consider for a vacation. He said the success of this trip had opened him up to considering a much broader range of places than he would have imagined before. I thought this meant anywhere from Ireland, or Paris, or Turkey. To Dino, it meant anywhere from Sorrento to Positano.

Maybe if they have grappa in Athens…

September 24: According to Dino

Cathy and I catch the boat to the airport and haul our newly expanded family of luggage down the dock. I give the evil eye to every porter who thinks that just because my wife is carrying, dragging, and kicking twice her body weight in luggage, I'm going to pay their ridiculous fees. Wrong. The airport is packed, and I thank God we can go to the expedited Delta Gold Medallion line. People in the normal line are still waiting to get on a plane as I write this.

We finally settle in and grab some duty-free salami and bottles of Bellini as we wait for our flight. It suddenly occurs to me that this is our last few minutes in Italy. Cathy reads a magazine, and I try to get into a book. Thirty pages in I realize I don't know what the hell I'm reading, so I give up and gaze off, thinking about the trip and how everyone did with the responsibilities they were originally assigned.

I have to admit that Cathy did her job extremely well. We had the best accommodations everywhere we went, had a great guide, and saw the most interesting sights. I also have to admit that I did a pretty good job learning the phrases we needed, and my ability to communicate in general was pretty damn good if I say so myself, (with those few previously noted exceptions—which weren't my fault).

Pete, as you recollect, was supposed to know the history. How did he do? Once, while we were strolling through Tuscany, I asked him what "Etruscan" was, and he said it was a kind of a bowl. He later told me he had bought a truscan and was thinking of buying some more truscans, but they were pretty expensive. Carolyn agreed. So much for Peter's research. I eventually learned not to ask him tough questions like, "Is it raining?" So I'd probably give him an F+. And Carolyn? Well, saying that she did a good job would be like saying that the farmer who got paid not to grow corn did a good job not growing the corn. In other words, things ended up exactly as I expected they would.

This isn't making me feel any better so I gaze out the window instead. I look at Italy. One last time. The land of my ancestors, the land of the best food in the world, the land of people who didn't get on the boat a hundred years ago like my grandparents did. These were the ones waving to them from the dock as they left their homes, looking forward to America, where the roads were paved with gold, or so they were told. Which ones made the right decisions? The ones who left, or the ones who stayed behind?

I guess like a lot of things, it depends. In our case, America was a good choice. The grandparents who came over became barbers and laborers, and the women worked ten-hour days on sewing machines, sitting next to their sisters and other minorities, Black, Polish, all kinds. They worked those machines with young, healthy hands and ended up with arthritic joints and deformed fingers. These people never complained, though, because they found the one thing that they came here seeking: opportunity. They had families during the Great Depression, but if you ask them there was nothing great about it. They learned how to make the most of what little they had. The hardships they endured formed qualities and principles that seemed corny to me when I was a kid. Things like saving your money, respecting other people, working hard, counting your blessings, and appreciating everything you had.

The grandparents had American-born kids, my dad and aunts and uncles. They had tough jobs, too. For most, college wasn't an option. For them, a good steady job was the goal. They were construction workers, teamsters, and waitresses. None of them complained about what wasn't fair, and no one thought anyone else owed them anything. They relied on themselves, and they relied on their families. And then they had kids.

For us, college wasn't just an option, it was expected. We got jobs and worked hard, too. But with college degrees, we didn't have to bust our asses pouring concrete on the roof of a Holiday Inn on Route 1 in ninety-five-degree heat. We had white-collar jobs. We competed with others who came from families with generational histories of white-collar jobs. But we competed, and we did well.

America. It's been a long ride, with each generation building on the hard work and sacrifice of the preceding generation. Families, staying together and looking out for each other. Keeping the traditions, the food, the language from the old country. Italy is in my blood. I don't really care that most of the Italians treated me like every other fookin tourist. To me, Italy was my country as much as it was theirs. But I must admit, we left it in good hands. I don't know what the Italy that my relatives left was like, but I know they'd be proud of what it is today. I had a great time here. I had my wonderful wife with me who appreciated everything as much as I did. We had another Italian-American couple with us, the Grecos, whose grandparents came to America years ago like the D'Adamos—maybe on the same boat. I doubt that either of them had balconies on that trip. And the Grecos had the same kind of century on American soil that we did. It *was* a land of opportunity. The roads weren't paved with gold, but they were paved by a lot of people with vowels at the ends of their names.

We board the plane and as I strap myself into my seat, I realize a lot of things that I didn't realize two weeks earlier, like Dorothy did. But I didn't have the Tin Man, I had Mario. I didn't have the Scarecrow, I had Vincenzo. I didn't have the Cowardly Lion, I had Enzo. I didn't have the Munchkins, I had the Grecos (who are about the same size), and I didn't have the Wicked Witch of Taiwan, I had Cathy. I finally get a hold of myself, realizing what a sorry, sentimental state I've sunken into as a result of spending two weeks with the Grecos, and I slowly drift off as the plane heads out over the Italian hills.

We get back home and have all of our pictures developed. Somehow our friends aren't as interested as we are in every shot and every detail describing where it was taken, what we were doing, the amusing anecdote, etc. Screw them.

Pete and I had a good shot at a book deal and we agreed that he would do the first part and I would add my version at the end.

I figured the reader would want to end on the funnier stuff. A few weeks later, Pete sent me a couple of days' of what he says happened. As I suspected, he screwed it up and got most of the details wrong. I added the accurate (and funny) version to the end and sent it back. Pretty soon we got ourselves a fookin book. We add some of our pictures, (not sure if the publisher will keep them in or not) throw in a couple of witty captions, and we're done. It ain't Hemingway, but neither is half the crap out there anyway, and who knows, people might actually buy it. Doesn't really matter because either way, I'm writing off the fucking trip.